# THE
# SPIRIT, SOUL
## AND
# BODY
## OF
# WORSHIP

Worshiping God with all we are

JOEL BALIN

# THE
# SPIRIT, SOUL
# AND
# BODY
# OF
# WORSHIP

Worshiping God with all we are

JOEL BALIN

ampelōn
PUBLISHING

Atlanta, GA

*To Trace Balin, my wife; Samuel Balin, my father; and Donnell Hemminger, my mentor. You have pointed the way for me in life, music, and the pursuit of learning and growing. Through your support and exhortation I've found myself, my calling, and my God.*

# CONTENTS

# ACKNOWLEDGEMENTS

This book is the culmination of 20 years of worshiping with God's people throughout the world. Their praises fill these pages.

• The worshipers at CrossBridge Church and the Atlanta Vineyard have shown me what it's like to worship with their whole hearts, minds, souls and strength in every circumstance. The people of Metro Life Church taught me how relationships and character determine our integrity in worship and the people of NorthGate church showed me how our passion and pursuit of God affects the depth of our worship. Thank you to Johnny Christ, Danny Jones, Mike Gilland and Marc Lawson for leading those people and leading me at pivotal junctures in my growth as a worshiper.

• My wife, Trace, has inspired and challenged me through her faithful dedication to God and me. My admiration for her writing and passion to creatively communicate all of God's facets knows no bounds. Her love sustains me.

• Kathy Smith's relentless pursuit of worshiping God with all her being has been a constant illustration that helped me refine and define my thoughts on worship and practices of living it out.

• I am profoundly grateful for Michael and Deb Goldstone, John and Marsha Moreland, and Todd and Anita Colwell who have helped me walk out a lifestyle of worship through authentic relationships and accountability.

• Casey Corum, Randy McCoy and the folks at Vineyard music have been a tremendous source of inspiration, friendship, and support in modeling stewardship of the extraordinary gifts and worship legacy they have been entrusted with.

• I am deeply appreciative of the contribution from my friends and co-laborers in ministry: Jane Joiner, Pat Brannon, John Morgan, Michelle Jolly, Jim Hettinger, Luane Thomson and Jeff Hayes. They have demonstrated an integrated worship life and provided a lab during our times together where my ideas on worship were incubated.

• I am very thankful for Angie Ramage for tirelessly working on the manuscript and getting so many of my thoughts on the page.

• I am immeasurably blessed by the constant encouragement, faithful friendship, and belief in me from Jason Chatraw and Dave Gilmore.

# Chapter One

# Kiss the Bride

### embracing intimacy in worship

*Then we shall see face to face. ... then I shall know fully,*
*even as I am fully known.*

1 CORINTHIANS 13:12

Throughout our involvement in music, music ministry, and worship leading, my wife Trace and I have traveled quite a bit. One of the most difficult things about traveling is trying to understand the customs of different cultures. Of course, as musicians we worked with other musicians, and that in itself is a culture shock of its own. On one flight, I was just getting settled in my seat when a flight attendant indicated over the intercom that they weren't going to be uptight and stuffy during our time on board. Since I want to lead people in worship that is not stuffy or uptight (while maintaining a godly reverence), I immediately "got on board" with their non-traditional antics. It especially hit home when she asked if any of the passengers knew the difference between a musician and a mutual fund. Everyone immediately understood when she shouted, "Eventually a mutual fund matures and makes money!" I constantly teach and exhort worship musicians toward maturity, but realize that there is a child-likeness to the wonder of worship that is important to maintain as well.

Walter was one such childlike musician. Once while sitting at dinner with the band Trace and I traveled with, Walter, our drummer, picked up his fork and started doing what any drummer would do with a fork. Not eating with it—banging things with it. Drummers are always banging on something, so it wasn't surprising when Walter hit his drinking glass—but then this look of revelation came over his face as and he blurted out, "Kiss the bride." We thought he was nuts. We laughed at poor Walter incessantly about his "kiss the bride" moment.

Years later I was attending a wedding reception, and to my amazement people began banging on their glasses with their forks and shouting, "Kiss the bride!" The groom willingly responded by leaning over and kissing his new bride. I knew something was up because they couldn't all be drummers. I never knew this was a real custom. I feel so badly for Walter, all the ridicule, the humiliation. If any of you happen to meet a drummer named Walter who starts banging on a glass, tell him that I'm really sorry.

But it's not during the tapping of the glasses at the wedding reception where the first signal is given to "kiss the bride." It's the time earlier when, as we all know, it is said by the pastor who is conducting the wedding ceremony. When he, at the long awaited moment, tells the groom, "You may now kiss the bride," the veil is lifted and the groom sees his bride face to face. It is at this time in the wedding ceremony that the bride and groom are able to kiss, to be intimate, because no veil separates them as it did before. This act is not only the most intimate time of the wedding ceremony, it represents an act of eternal significance. Just as it seals a covenant between the husband and wife, it also demonstrates a covenant between us, the bride of Christ, and the Lord.

When officiating weddings, I often paraphrase Ephesians 5 by saying "A groom is to love his bride as Christ loves the church and is to give himself for her just as Jesus gave himself for us as His bride." God so longs for an intimate relationship with us that He was willing to allow His only son to die to tear down every barrier between Him and us. Matthew 27:51 says that when Christ died on the cross, "the veil of the temple was torn in two from top to bottom." The whole of history pointed to this time when God lifted the veil that had separated us from Jesus and said to His Son, "You may now kiss the Bride." This was God's way of saying that we were no longer separated from Him. We could enter into His holiest of places and not only worship Him, but experience unhindered, unveiled, intimate love. Now when I hear someone drum on their glass with a fork and shout, "Kiss the bride!", I think of God signaling us to worship Him intimately and unveiled with nothing separating us from Him.

As believers, we are a part of the body of Christ—His bride— and there will be a time at His coming when all of heaven is shouting, "Kiss the bride!" But we don't have to wait until eternity to worship the Lord intimately. We can do this right now— right where we are today.

## YOU MAKE ME FEEL LIKE A NATURAL ... WORSHIPER

To some, worship seems like an isolated, detached-from-normal-life activity relegated to Sunday mornings in church. Yet worship is the most universal and natural activity we could do as human beings. We were created to worship. Everyone worships. The question is not will we worship, but who or what will we worship? What captures your attention, your heart, your affection? What consumes your time or maintains your interest? I'm not saying that anything we spend time on or are interested in is an idol that we worship, but unless we focus our deepest affections and desires on God, we are really worshiping something else.

15

Just as our bodies need water and food for sustenance, our spirits and souls need the life sustaining presence of God through worship. Yet, many of us who wouldn't dream of missing a meal, going days without connecting with or failing to think about the Lord and what He has done for us. In this first chapter, I want to lay a foundation for worship as a natural part of our everyday lives, or as the Bible tells us, "So here's what I want you to do, God helping you: Take your everyday, ordinary life—your sleeping, eating, going-to-work, and walking-around life—and place it before God as an offering" (Romans 12:1, The Message).

In *That Incredible Christian*, A. W. Tozer wrote, "We are called to an everlasting preoccupation with God." This means that while we may go through our days working, talking with others, and following a routine, we also are called by God to be mindful of Him—to consider Him in all that we do and say. King David was consumed with love for and worship of the Lord. Solomon wrote volumes dedicated to the glory of the Lord and intimacy with the King. Abraham vowed to go wherever the Lord led him simply because He was determined to follow the One who had captured his heart. Paul and Silas, though imprisoned, worshiped the Lord and experienced God's freedom. The Bible and history are filled with men and women like these who were caught up in total devotion to God. Their testimonies are of lives filled with worship and praise often in the midst of immense personal suffering. They determined to draw close to God. But this wasn't always true of the people God had chosen to call His own. The Bible tells of generations who lived in slavery and were separated from the Lord's presence, glory and intimate love ... until Moses sang God's victory chant, "Let My people go."

The Israelites finally got out of Egypt, but they still needed to learn to trust and worship God fully. Like He does during our desert experiences, God used their time in the desert to remove all that they relied on or thought was valuable in order to give them something of eternal value.

In the desert, rather than complain or turn to idols, Moses met with God. He tenaciously sought God out. The Lord would speak to Moses face to face, as a man speaks with his friend. (Exodus 33:11) Moses asked God to teach him His ways so he would know Him. So, God said to Moses, "I will do the very thing you have asked, because I am pleased with you and I know you by name." (Exodus 33:17) When Moses returned from being on Mt. Sinai with God, his face glowed from having seen the glory of the Lord.

The sight of Moses with his face all aglow frightened the Israelites:

> When Moses came down from Mount Sinai with the two tablets of the Testimony in his hands, he was not aware that his face was radiant because he had spoken with the Lord. When Aaron and all the Israelites saw Moses, his face was radiant, and they were afraid to come near him. . . . When Moses finished speaking to them, he put a veil over his face. But whenever he entered the Lord's presence to speak with him, he removed the veil until he came out.
>
> – Exodus 34:29-30; 33-34

In 2 Corinthians, Paul explains the reality of this event, "Even to this day when Moses is read, a veil covers their hearts. But whenever anyone turns to the Lord, the veil is taken away. Now the Lord is the Spirit, and where the Spirit of the Lord is, there is freedom" (2 Corinthians 3:16-17). Paul describes here the difference between the bondage of hiding behind the rules and regulations of the Law rather than the freedom of an unveiled intimate relationship with God.

In the Middle East the wearing of a veil is customary. For many cultures, it is shameful for a woman to allow another man, other than her husband, to gaze on her face. Even today in many Middle Eastern cultures this is still true. Women simply do not appear in public without their faces being covered. The intimacy of an unveiled face is reserved for a woman's husband and not for a public setting. While this way of thinking is changing, it can help us understand the concept the people of the Bible had of being veiled from intimacy.

The Jews in the Old and New Testaments were familiar with another use of a veil as a means of separation. In the temple, a veil was used to separate the people from the most holy place. Only the high priest was allowed to enter the Holy of Holies once a year on the Day of Atonement. This chamber symbolized the closest place on earth to God. It also was a place of divine intimacy but not for the common man or woman. The veil and the law kept people from a close personal relationship with God.

As believers, our veils have been lifted, and there are now no barriers between us and Christ. Once we accept Him as our Savior and ask Him to forgive our sins and cleanse our hearts, we are united with Him for eternity. We are His and we are betrothed to Him. The most intimate worship songs in the Bible are found in "Song of Songs." Speaking of a young maiden (the church) and her beloved (Christ), it allegorically describes our relationship with phrases like, "I am my beloved's and my beloved is mine" (Song of Songs 6:3). Approaching an "R" rating for its overt description of sensual love, Song of Songs depicts an untainted, uncovered, unveiled intimacy that existed between Adam and Eve and God before the fall. When we approach God in worship with our hearts and lives uncovered and unveiled, we can enjoy the relationship He originally designed for us to have with Him.

> As believers, our veils have been lifted, and there are now no barriers between us and Christ.

## FEAR FACTOR

Starting a few years ago, I have prayed that I would be free from the destructive fear of man and any other carnal fear and become filled with the life giving fear of the Lord. True worship requires a healthy, reverent fear of the Lord. However, this fear is not the fear that the world experiences. It is a reverent fear that leads to an awesome sense of love and devotion to God. Moses wrote, "Hear, O Israel: The Lord our God, the Lord is one. Love the Lord your God with all your heart and with all your soul and with all your strength," (Deuteronomy 6:4-5). It's not surprising that the same guy who penned these words was also the one who stood in God's presence until he glowed! The Bible tells us that after Moses talked with God, his appearance was so astounding that Aaron ordered that a veil be placed over Moses' face. A few verses later, Moses admonishes us to "Fear the Lord your God." There's no doubt that fear plays an important role in worship. We can either reverently fear the Lord in the glory of His presence as Moses did, or we can have the run-and-hide fear that has kept people from true worship for centuries.

One of the most menacing things that fear does is to cause people to focus on what they don't have or will not have and to stop praising the Lord for what He has done in their lives. In other words, fear actually prevents worship and praise. Instead of motivating us to sing songs with an attitude of gratitude to the Lord, it can cause our hearts to go cold, produce feelings of anxiety instead of God's peace, and cloud our minds with thoughts that do not reflect God's love for us.

The type of fear that Moses was writing about, however, was an awesome fear of the Lord that leads to a deeper sense of worship and love. It is a fear that brings a sense of true humility and worship of God. We bow down in fear not because we are frightened but because his awesome presence so compels us to worship

Him that there is nothing left for us to do but to praise Him with all that we are—spirit, soul, and body.

The Israelites had never seen the glory of the Lord. However, when Moses returned from receiving the Ten Commandments, they saw his glowing countenance and were afraid. Likewise, when a storm erupted out on the open Sea of Galilee, the disciples were afraid. They were seasoned fishermen, but the fierceness of a storm's raging wind and waves caused their hearts to melt. When they saw the Lord walking toward them, they at first felt panic. But when Jesus stepped into their boat and commanded the elements of nature to be still, their attention turned to Him, and they fell on their faces in worship.

While holy fear draws us to and connects us with God, carnal fear separates us from God. Like the Israelites, when we try to approach God based on keeping the rules and regulations—the Law—we can never possibly measure up. Therefore, when we are in God's presence, we are afraid, expecting to be punished for not being perfect. But when we approach God in love, knowing that He accepts us not because of our own righteousness but in the righteousness Christ provided for us, we can come to Him without fear separating us. John, who was Jesus' closest friend on earth, understood being close to Jesus meant receiving His love. Three times the Bible calls him "the disciple whom Jesus loved." He wrote these words, "There is no fear in love. But perfect love drives out fear, because fear has to do with punishment" (1 John 4:18).

The New Living Translation says, "If we are afraid, it is for fear of judgment"—but every judgment that we deserve was taken to the cross and fully satisfied in Christ. And that is why we can, "approach the throne of grace with confidence" (Hebrews 4:16). Think of how it would separate you from your spouse or friends if every time you were with them you wore a curtain over your face. Not only would they think you were weird, it would destroy any ability to truly connect. That is the way it is if we come before God in carnal fear rather than love.

One six-year-old girl runs up to her father with the picture she drew. He says in elation, "Wow, honey, that's the most beautiful pony I've ever seen. I just love it when you draw for me." Another child the same age reluctantly hands her father a drawing and then cowers in fear as he says, "That's the worst drawing I have ever seen. It looks like more like a stupid rabbit than a horse. Until you learn to draw, I don't want to see any of these lame attempts at art."

Which child are you? Which father do you see in God? Do you think that He loves you so deeply that He delights in your offering even though you are not perfect, or do you think He rejects you because you don't measure up? The way you see God will determine your ability to get close to Him in worship.

It was an unhealthy sense of fear that drove man from God. However, it is the "right" view of fear that brings us back. While God wants us to reverently fear Him, His greatest desire is that we learn to love Him and walk in worship of Him daily. When we learn how to praise God for His goodness, faithfulness, and abiding love, we will experience freedom from legalistic fear and any other spiritual bondage that has a grip on our lives. Worshiping with our entire being brings us into the presence of God where His spirit reminds us of the truth of God that sets us free. (John 8:32)

## TRUTH OR CONSEQUENCES

God wants us to worship in truth with our spirit, soul, and body. This is what brings us into intimacy with Him. My prayer is for the Lord to instill in us His plan for worship in the church today and for our personal lives so that our hearts will be made like His, our spirits will commune with His, and our character will reflect the goodness of His love.

In order for this to happen, we need to be aligned with the truth while experiencing freedom in the Spirit. However, if we are afraid, as Israel was at the sight of Moses' face, then we risk missing a divine opportunity to build an intimate relationship with the Savior. You don't have to cave into fear or be bound by religious tradition. Some traditions lead to a deeper sense of worship. But if these are not balanced with the truth of God's present grace, they can become burdensome requirements or routines that actually keep us from God rather than connecting us to Him. But Jesus tore in two the veil that once separated us from a Holy God. Let's not put the veil back over us by being afraid to come openly and honestly before God, bringing our weaknesses, asking for forgiveness of our sins and offering ourselves to Him.

Since Jesus provided the way, we can, "Worship the Lord with gladness; come before him with joyful songs. Know that the Lord is God. It is he who made us, and we are his; we are his people, the sheep of his pasture. Enter his gates with thanksgiving and his courts with praise; give thanks to him and praise his name. For the Lord is good and his love endures forever; his faithfulness continues through all generations" (Psalm 100: 2-5).

What are the results of fully worshiping God?

*First, we experience the wonder of being in His presence.* The fact is that we always are in the presence of God, but through worship we become keenly aware of who He is and actually enjoy Him as He enjoys our worship of Him. Through worship we can engage in and experience, "Man's chief and highest end ... to glorify God, and fully to enjoy him forever." (Westminster Catechisms)

*Second, we gain a tremendous sense of peace and joy.* We draw near to the heart of God and realize that He is near to us. When we approach God in worship, we are drawn to him like a magnet. He is the most positive force in the universe and our humility represents the opposite end of the magnet that is drawn to and connected with the powerful love of God. When we are connected in this way, nothing can separate us from the love of God, and our music and worship conveys the love and peace of His presence to everyone gathered in our churches.

*Third, we can rest.* Worship provides the opportunity we need to rest in Christ and allow His intimate love to carry us. Isaiah wrote, "This is the resting place, let the weary rest" (Isaiah 28:12). At first glance, we might think that the prophet was talking about "taking a break." After all, isn't that what rest is all about?

In this context, the word rest does not necessarily mean a rest from work or activity but, instead, trusting in the Lord. When we rest in Christ, we place our trust and faith in His eternal care. We allow Him to take care of us and provide for every need we have. This relationship of faith, trust and worship is what God wanted for the people of Israel. But later in this chapter, God said that they were only interested in following their laws and tradition.

Instead of resting in God, Israel's own fear-based self-effort was causing many of the problems they were facing. They were blinded to the truth, therefore, their hearts were separated from the Lord. The Lord draws us unto Himself so that He can speak to us and demonstrate His love to us. Then our hearts will be filled with the right motivation for worship. Living by the law and tradition never leads to true worship.

Israel refused to rest in God's care and presence and as a result of their disobedience the word of the Lord to them became, "do and do, do and do, rule on rule, rule on rule" (Isaiah 28:13). The Hebrew words for these phrases are "Sav La Sav, Kav La Kav," which is more of a mocking sound than an actual statement—kind of like "Yada, Yada, Yada." It is as though God was looking down at them and saying, "You foolish children. You have chosen rules and regulations over an intimate relationship with Me." Sadly, many times, He could say the same of us. But this is not the route

23

you have to take. God has a better way and you can experience the wonder of His presence through worship and praise.

There are tremendously important traditions within the Christian church—ones that are foundational to our faith. But tradition alone does not lead us to a point of heartfelt worship. Praise and adoration to Jesus Christ does, and this is God's goal for your life. He seeks your heartfelt love and adoration. He accepts you and loves you just the way you are. If there are changes that need to take place in your life, He will work on those, but first do this above all else: Seek His kingdom and worship only Him. (Matthew 6:33)

## THE POINT OF THE STORY

We were created by God to enjoy His fellowship. Intimacy comes through worship and praise as we enter into His presence with a heart of thanksgiving. Singer and worship leader, Matt Redman says, "Intimacy is all about self disclosure, which means revealing something of yourself to someone else. As we reveal the secret places of our hearts to God, He reveals the secret things of His heart to us. When this happens, there's exchange of love between a Holy, righteous God and us. ... This is the relationship that we could describe as intimacy."

The point of the "kiss the bride" story at the beginning of this chapter has only one purpose: God wants to be our intimate Lord and Savior. He wants to lift the veil off of our eyes so that we may see Him and worship Him and experience the unconditional love that He has for us. The people of Israel were afraid when they saw Moses' face, but we do not have to be afraid to approach God's throne of mercy and grace. While the face of Moses was veiled, we can look to God unveiled for the Lord has provided freedom as we turn to Him through Christ.

The apostle Paul writes, "Even to this day when Moses is

read, a veil covers their hearts. But whenever anyone turns to the Lord, the veil is taken away. Now the Lord is the Spirit, and where the Spirit of the Lord is, there is freedom. And we, who with unveiled faces all reflect the Lord's glory are being transformed into his likeness with ever-increasing glory, which comes from the Lord, who is the Spirit" (2 Corinthians 3:15-18).

In his book, *The Purpose Driven Life*, author Rick Warren explains God so longed for an intimate relationship with us that He sent His Son to die for our sins saying, "I'd rather die than live without you," and He did. When Christ died, the veil separating us from eternal life with God was lifted. Sin's power was broken and every barrier that the enemy of our souls had erected in an effort to separated us from God was torn down.

The phrase, "you may now kiss the bride," contains an intimacy that one day will be realized as we see Jesus Christ face to face. However, even today—this moment and this hour—worship brings us to a place where we can experience intimate relationship with God. Because He is the One who has lifted the veil, there is now nothing to prevent us from knowing Him and experiencing His love, forgiveness, and grace.

## WORSHIP AS A LIFESTYLE

A chief characteristic of Jesus and a prerequisite to worship is humility. A humble and contrite heart can only lead to one place and that is a place of worship. These are the characteristics that God loves to see in the life of a believer. (Isaiah 66:2) Mary demonstrated this when she anointed Jesus before His death. "Mary took about a pint of pure nard, an expensive perfume; she poured it on Jesus' feet and wiped his feet with her hair. And the house was filled with the fragrance of the perfume" (John 12:3). In other words, Mary worshiped Jesus, was broken before Him and a glorious fragrance filled the place.

As a worship leader, it's easy for me to focus my worship experience on what happens when we sing and play on Sunday mornings. But worship is really about our whole life "poured out" before God as a fragrant offering. Mary held nothing back in her display of love for Jesus. The oil that she poured on Christ's feet was very costly. It represented a lifetime of wages, but this meant nothing to her compared to the opportunity to worship her Lord.

Songwriter and worship leader, Brian Doerksen writes, "Intimacy in the 'narrow' sense means we sing to God. In the broad sense, intimacy means we live our whole lives in the presence of God. If we give ourselves away to other loves and other gods, we will lose intimacy with God, or we will try to manufacture it in a way that is shallow and purely physical. This leads to an empty encounter for both God and us. ... We cannot spend our entire week in pursuit of the world and then wonder why our worship on Sunday feels flat. Real intimacy cannot be created by simply singing the right songs. Intimate worship really happens when the songs come as an overflow of a heart full of love. ... Intimate worship will always be our highest calling and aim in this life, and then, when we pass on to the other side, it's only going to get better."

True worship is:

• *an offering of ourselves to the Lord.* In Romans, Paul writes, "Offer your bodies as living sacrifices, holy and pleasing to God— this is your spiritual act of worship. " (Romans 12:1).

• *love responding to love.* "We love because he first loved us" (1 John 4:19). God's love for us is so great that He sent His Son to die for us. There is no greater love than this. Worship doesn't start with us; it is initiated by God lavishing on us eternal love. It is manifest when we recognize and receive that love and respond by loving God in return through worshiping with a thankful heart.

You will never find the face of Christ veiled or hidden from your view. He wants you to be intimate with Him as His bride without a veil covering your face. If there is something that is separating you from Him, take it to the foot of His Cross and leave it there. His forgiveness is eternal and His love for you is everlasting.

*Father, gather me in Your arms and take me to Your intimate place of worship. Teach my heart to sing a new song as I live my life for You. (Psalm 96:1-2)*

# Chapter Two

# A Pure Reflection

keeping the main thing the main thing

*Let the word of Christ dwell in you richly ...*
*as you sing psalms, hymns and spiritual songs*
*with gratitude in your hearts to God.*

COLOSSIANS 3:16

A ll of us could probably make a list of things that can distract us from worship: entertainment, our jobs, relationships issues, personal ambitions, money, material possessions and many more. Anything that prevents us from giving ourselves totally and completely to the Lord can and usually does hinder worship. Does this mean that we need to stop what we are doing and only spend time in worship? No, but it does mean that for us to have hearts of worship and praise, our lives need to have a God-centered focus.

Author and pastor Louie Giglio emphasizes, "Worship is a way of life. It is the air [we] breath. However, if we yield to idolatry, we simply exchange the Creator for something created." The truth is very simple. We may not bow down before a statue, but we are very capable of bowing our knees and giving our attention to feelings of pride, the desire for money, and better positions in society and at work. We race after the latest entertainment gear and hurry to enlist ourselves and families in all kinds of activities that at times distract us from and prevent us from worshiping the Lord.

A number of years ago my wife and I were traveling on the road, singing and ministering in various churches. We had bought an old motor home and were on our way to do a concert when the furnace went out. The main unit was located under one of the seats and I decided to take a look to see if I could find out what was wrong. When I lifted the cover, I found something that blew us away. It was a book entitled *God's Missionary* by Amy Carmichael.

When Trace opened the pages of this little book and read the words that had been written by a woman who had dedicated her entire life rescuing, serving and discipling others, I was stirred. Amy Carmichael's life was one of sacrifice and dedication to God. As a young woman, she left her home in England and never returned, but chose, instead, to remain in Dohnavur, India, where with God's help she established places of safety and refuge for children whose lives were in danger.

In *God's Missionary*, she writes, "Anything that would hinder us from the closest walk that is possible to us till we see Him face to face is not for us. We need to be sensitive to the first approach of the hindering thing. For the sake of the souls that may be stumbled if we turn even ever so little aside, for the sake of our Master's glory—dearer surely to us than all else—let us ask Him now to show us whether in anywise we have been following 'crooked patterns.'"

For months, Trace and I feasted on this quote. Like the widow in Luke 21, we wanted to give every ounce of what we had to the Lord for His glory. Jesus noted that this woman gave "all that she had." From the world's perspective, it may have seemed like a small sum, but from God's perspective, it was a gift of abundant wealth because it was given sacrificially with a heart of love.

You may feel as though you do not have much to offer God. He is not looking for a huge quantity; He is looking for a huge heart-devotion. When you give what you have whether it is time, talent, or money, He is glorified and worship takes place. Give yourself to God and you will have a sense of wealth that cannot be purchased by this world.

## EXPERIENCING TRANSFORMATION

God created us to worship Him, but the things of this world constantly compete for our affection. This is why Jesus told the people to love the Lord with all their hearts. He was giving them a commandment, but it was not to establish more law; rather it was to lead them to an intimate relationship with God. In the book of Romans, Paul takes this concept a step further, "I urge you, brothers, in the view of God's mercy, to offer your bodies as living sacrifices, holy and pleasing to God—this is your spiritual act of worship. Do not conform any longer to the pattern of this world, but be transformed by the renewing of your mind. Then you will be able to test and approve what God's will is—his good, pleasing and perfect will" (12:1-2).

Paul wrote these words to a group of people who had their priorities out of balance. Most of those in the New Testament church had come out of a pagan lifestyle. Their minds, however, were being "transformed" by God's grace along with their emotions and actions. They no longer worshiped "other" gods. Instead, they were learning to worship the One true God—the very person who had saved them from their sins. Their eternal transformation from a heavenly standpoint was instantaneous. However, there were habits that needed changing. They needed to be reminded to keep the focus of their hearts set on the Lord

Jesus. This was the "main thing" that needed to take place.

Early Christians, like us, had to learn how to worship God and how to live their lives for Him each day. God is patient and long-suffering. He is willing to teach us all that we need to know about worship—even if it takes a lifetime to learn. Many of us think of worship as something that only takes place in church, but worship is much broader than this. It is an experience and expression of the deepest part of our being and meant to be lived out through every part of our lives.

In Colossians, Paul tells us to "let the word of Christ dwell in [us] richly . . . as [we] sing psalms, hymns and spiritual songs with gratitude in [our] hearts to God" (3:16). The key to worship is getting your heart right before Him.

How do you do this?

• *Ask God to give you the right image of who He is.* Many people do not know how to worship the Lord because they have a false or flawed image of Him. He is an omniscient God who knows you completely yet loves you eternally, and accepts you just the way you are through Jesus. No one will ever love you more or care about you more than He does. However, past hurts and disappointments can distort your view of God and hinder your worship of Him, especially when you fail to see God's grace being poured out over your life in these times of pain. Worship opens our eyes to the reality of God's ever present love that heals our hearts, forgives our sins and empowers us to live beyond our circumstances!

Legalism and stale religious traditionalism can also keep us from worshiping God freely. Many of the rituals we practice in our churches date back to New Testament times and can lead to meaningful worship and praise. However, they can become a blockage when we just go through the familiar motions of tradition. God desires Worshipers who will allow the Spirit to permeate their traditions with meaning, passion and fresh expressions.

In other words, allow God to have complete access to your worship. Be open and sensitive to the active presence of the Holy Spirit, especially in times of worship.

• *Surrender your life to Christ.* If we refuse to give our entire lives and hearts to God, it hinders our worship. Even Jesus willingly surrendered to His heavenly Father. When we raise our hands in worship, it not only symbolizes that we are children lifting our hands up to our Heavenly Father, but it also signifies the act of surrender to our Lord.

Paul says that the entirety of our lives should be an act of worship in loving surrender to God. He was underscoring what Jesus told His followers—"Love the Lord your God with all your heart and with all your soul and with all your mind and with all your strength" (Matthew 22:37).

Too often, our worship and affection is directed toward the things of this world and not God. We become entangled with the values of a godless society that does not have its focus set on Christ. This is one of the reasons we find worship and praise to God difficult. The question isn't if we will worship, but who or what we worship. We were designed to worship, and unless God is the object of our worship, something else will be.

The Greek word for "worship" is *proskenuo.* It literally means "to turn and kiss." It means to be willing to turn away from the temporal love of the world and turn toward the eternal love of the Lord in an intimate and affectionate way.

## UNVEILED FACES

Those of us who are worship leaders have the wondrous opportunity to lead people from the glory of God's throne room to the intimacy of His embrace. We are attendants to the bride of Christ, helping prepare her to be a radiant reflection of the groom's love. As we "behold the Lord" with our faces unveiled, we can proclaim along with John the Baptist, who "saw Jesus coming to him and said, 'Behold, the Lamb of God who takes away the sin of the world!'" (John 1:29, NASB).

In 2 Corinthians 3:18, Paul writes, "We all, with unveiled face, beholding as in a mirror the glory of the Lord, are being transformed into the same image from glory to glory, just as from the Lord, the Spirit." God is changing us into people who know, love, and worship Him.

"Beholding as in a mirror" connotes reflecting as well as looking into. As we behold the glory of the Lord, we gaze at Him and His beauty and are transformed into His image by the Spirit of the Lord. We then reflect the glory and image of Christ that we behold.

We come into God's presence through worship, praise, and prayer, but we do not emerge the same. As we behold God, we are transformed into those who reflect His beauty and character. We don't have to wait for heaven before we can experience God's glory. God continually reaches out to each one of us through the Holy Spirit—drawing us closer to Himself, showing us more of Himself and making us more like Himself.

God's desire is still the same as when He revealed Himself to Isaiah. He wants to fill the temple with his presence. (Isaiah 6:1; 1 Kings 8:10) Because we are the temple of God, He comes to fill us. He wants to live in us, not just visit our building on Sunday morning: "Don't you know that you yourselves are God's temple and that God's Spirit lives in you?" (1 Corinthians 3:16). Jesus does not come to us for a visitation; He comes for habitation, to dwell in us. When our hearts are aligned with His we can sing with all our hearts, minds, soul, and strength this line from the song "Dwell":

*Dwell in the midst of us, come and have Your way.*

When we do, we will discover that God "will take great delight in you, he will quiet you with his love, he will rejoice over you with singing" (Zephaniah 3:17).

*Lord, I want to worship you in spirit and in truth so that every area of my life reflects a part of You to others. I lift my face up to You, Lord Jesus. Dwell in me today and forever and dwell in the midst of us as we gather for your Glory.*

# Chapter Three

# Barrier Grief

## breaking the unsound barriers

*I will praise the Lord, who counsels me;*
*even at night my heart instructs me.*
*I have set the Lord always before me.*
*Because he is at my right hand,*
*I will not be shaken.*
*Therefore my heart is glad and my tongue rejoices.*

PSALMS 16:7-9

Once while I was waiting to pay for an item at a local music store, a clerk began talking to the guy in line in front of me. He explained that whenever he went home his girlfriend was "all over his case" to get married. In frustration the clerk said, "I just don't understand. Why does she want to get married?" I caught the idea that this guy was living with his girlfriend, so I spoke up with "I do." He looked at me as I came closer to the counter and said, "You do what?", to which I replied, "I understand why she wants to get married."

I began to explain that from what I heard him saying, he wanted his girlfriend to "be there" for him. He wanted her to be faithful, affectionate, and supportive. He wanted her time, her undivided love and even her body to which he responded with a hardy agreement. I pointed out that it was amazing that he wanted this type of commitment but could not respond to her with a similar commitment in marriage. He had this puzzled look on his face as he told me that he'd never seen it that way.

## NOW I UNDERSTAND

As Christians, so often we eagerly look for God to demonstrate His affection toward us. We expect Him to be faithful to give His life to us. But are we as faithful to make the commitment to give ourselves that fully to Him? We may reserve our lives for ourselves and hold back our love and affection. Jesus, however, held nothing back. He gave His body for us; He gave His very life. But it wasn't so that we could have a casual relationship.

> Jesus is not coming back for a "girlfriend"; He is coming back for a bride!

Jesus is not coming back for a "girlfriend"; He is coming back for a bride! He doesn't just want to move in with us; He wants a marriage where we are one with Him.

Are you holding back or hesitating in your devotion to the Lord? The depth of your worship is often a telltale sign of the level of your personal commitment to God. In the book *Tozer on Worship and Entertainment*, A. W. Tozer writes, "If you do not worship God seven days a week, you do not worship Him on one day a week. There is no such thing known in heaven as Sunday worship unless it is accompanied by Monday worship and Tuesday worship and so on. ... Ask the Lord to permeate your whole life with a spirit of worship—all week long, every day."

One thing we need to remember is that we are to worship God with all that we are. We do not have to spend hours on our knees in prayer and praise in order to worship Him, but we do need to have hearts totally devoted to Him. Worship isn't just about singing with a group of people at a service. We can worship and even sing to the Lord in our cars on the way to the office or the store. We also can worship Him while lying in our beds as King David often did. (Psalm 63:6) Ask the Lord to help you to begin to practice being in His presence. Once you learn to do this, worship will overflow from every area of your life. Brother Lawrence writes in his book *The Practice of the Presence of God* about his life of simply abiding continually with the Lord: "There is not in the world a kind of life more sweet and delightful than that of a continual conversation with God. Those only can comprehend it who practice and experience it." May we practice it and experience it.

We would probably all like a continual closeness with the Lord but there are barriers to that kind of worship. Before we can praise the Lord freely, we need to face and deal with them. However, for every barrier, God has a "break through" strategy. He knows our weaknesses and strengths. He also has a plan for accomplishing His purposes in our lives. But we must be willing to take the first step by seeking His love, forgiveness, mercy, and grace.

What are the potential barriers in your life? There may be many. I believe there are five that have the potential to prevent us from doing what God created us to do—spending time with Him in worship, prayer, and praise. As you read over the following list, ask God to help you identify any that may be in your life. Then be willing to surrender your heart to Him in these areas. When you do, He will tear down and eliminate all that prevents you from entering His holy place of worship.

• **Shame.** I have chosen to list shame before sin because it has the potential to keep us from coming to God in the repentance, worship, prayer, and fellowship that frees us from our sin. When we live in shame, we want to keep our sin (and consequently ourselves) hidden from God. It can tempt us to believe a lie—one that says we can't let anyone, even God, see who we truly are because if they do, they will reject us.

God will never reject you! He created you and loves you. Shame also tempts us to think that there is something fundamentally wrong—something that makes us unacceptable to the Lord and others. This is one of the enemy's darkest lies. He knows that God accepts us unconditionally and wants to tempt us to doubt the Lord's goodness. The truth is that God loves us with an everlasting love. (Jeremiah 31:3) While He doesn't accept our sin, He certainly accepts us. Therefore, we do not have to be ashamed to come into His presence. When the enemy tempts us to believe a lie, we must remember that nothing is strong enough to separate us from God's love.

*You can overcome shame.* One of the most important truths to remember is that God loves and accepts you. (Romans 15:7) A lady that I know was living with her boyfriend when God began to tug at her heart. She really wanted to be a part of the church community but felt as though she would not be accepted. Once she began to visit our church, God lined up the right people to reach out to her and an amazing thing happened. She began to desire a relationship with the Lord.

Over a few months, I watched her life turn around as God's grace was poured out to her through others. As she began to understand just how much the Lord loved her and that He had created her for a purpose, she couldn't help but give herself to Him. Her life changed. She got married, and she became a beautiful believer and follower of Jesus Christ. Worship is a very integral part of allowing people to taste what God is like. When people see the beauty of the Lord through worship, they will recognize Him through the messages we preach, the songs we sing, and the care that we demonstrate.

Jesus is never ashamed of you. The author of Hebrews writes, "Both the one who makes men holy and those who are made holy are of the same family. So Jesus is not ashamed to call them brothers" (Hebrews 2:11). Learn to agree with God and not the enemy about who you are in Christ. You are a child of God, saved by His grace, and loved eternally. Anytime you hear words like, "You are a failure, worthless, hopeless, and you will never change," rebuke these thoughts. This is the enemy's condemnation, and it is not God who is doing the talking! He will never tear you down; He only lifts you up. (Psalm 30:11) He will convict you of sin, but He will also provide the motivation and grace you need to step out of any wrong situation. The condemnation of shame says to cover your sin because it makes you unlovable and unforgivable; the conviction of the Holy Spirit says you are loved, so bring your sin to God in repentance and be forgiven.

Your name is written on the palm of His hand, and just like Jacob, you are the apple of God's eye. (Deuteronomy 32:10) You can put on the pure, white wedding dress that is reserved for the bride of Christ because you are just that—His bride!

• **Sin.** Sin is a major barrier to worship and intimacy with God. God knows the devastating effect sin has on us and that it separates us from Him. Sin is such a barrier to our relationship with God that He gave up his only Son to free us from it. When Jesus died, he tore the veil that separates us from God. When we sin, it pulls the veil back over our faces. We cannot be close to God while harboring unconfessed sin.

Worship is offering ourselves to God. Paul told the church in Rome, "Do not offer the parts of your body to sin, as instruments of wickedness, but rather offer yourselves to God" (Romans 6:13).

When we come to Christ and accept Him as our Savior, we are united with God and our sins are forgiven. The veil that once covered our faces is lifted, and we are freed to experience God's love and worship. (Isaiah 53:12) However, if we return to sin and yield to it, our faces will become spiritually veiled again. After David committed adultery with Bathsheba, God convicted him of his sin. Even though he was a man "after God's own heart" (Acts 13:22), David had to confess his deliberate failure to the Lord or suffer the consequences of broken fellowship with the God he loved. In Psalm 51 David prayed, "Have mercy on me, O God, according to your unfailing love; according to your great compassion blot out my transgressions. Wash away all my iniquity and cleanse me from my sin. For I know my transgressions, and my sin is always before me. Against you, you only, have I sinned and done what is evil in your sight ... Create in me pure heart, O God, and renew a steadfast spirit within me. Do not cast me from your presence or take your Holy Spirit from me. Restore to me the joy of your salvation and grant me a willing spirit, to sustain me" (vs.1-4; 10-11).

While there were consequences to David's sin, God's mercy and grace sustained him and the blessings of the Lord were his once again to enjoy.   And the result David said would come of being cleansed from His sin through confession and repentance was that "my tongue will sing of your righteousness ... my mouth will declare your praise" (Psalms 51:14-15).

Never allow unconfessed sin to prevent you from experiencing all that God has for you. You have a choice. Sin does not have to rob you of your worship, joy, and praise; and it certainly does not have the right to keep you from the loving presence of a holy God. David lived his life with an attitude of wanting to please only God.  He knew that a heart of worship was born and nurtured in unbroken fellowship and worship with a holy God. "Search me, O God," David prayed, "and know my heart; test me and know my anxious thoughts. See if there is any offensive way in me, and lead me in the way everlasting" (Psalm 139:23).

*You can overcome sin.* D.L. Moody tells us to "keep a short account" of sin. In other words, don't cover up sin thinking it will go away because it won't. As a worship leader, I have seen people really struggle with this. They come to church on Sunday longing to praise and worship the Lord, but unconfessed sin has placed a covering of guilt and shame over their lives. They try to worship but end up feeling unacceptable to God.

Whenever the Holy Spirit convicts you of something that you have done wrong, stop immediately and confess it to the Lord. Don't give the enemy an inch. He loves to condemn and berate the believer. However, Paul writes in Romans, "There is now no condemnation for those who are in Christ Jesus" (8:1). Therefore, you can go to God in prayer and be confident that He hears not only your audible words but also the silent cries of your heart.

God has a simple but remarkable two-step solution for sin. *First, we need to confess it.* You can go to Him in prayer anytime and anywhere and receive His forgiveness and grace. The Bible tells us "if we confess our sins, he is faithful and just and will forgive us our sins and purify us from all unrighteousness" (1 John 1:9). Transparency in worship comes as a result of true confession and humility.

*Second, repent from all known sin.* This means to turn away from the things that would keep us from God's fellowship. Paul writes, "Repent, then, and turn to God, so that your sins may be wiped out, that times of refreshing may come from the Lord" (Acts 3:19). In the Garden of Eden, Adam and Eve enjoyed unbroken fellowship with God. While sin disrupted this, God provided a covering for their transgressions just as He has provided one for us through Jesus Christ.

The solution to sin and forgiveness is simple. However, because the enemy has veiled the eyes of those who are lost, taking the first step toward freedom can be difficult. But it is necessary! Satan will try every tactic he can to keep us from taking the right steps toward an intimate relationship with the Lord Jesus Christ. Once we are saved by God's grace, he continues his tactics. Even the apostle Paul felt pressure in this area. However, he knew the power of God to deliver him and we can, too! He wrote, "Who will rescue me from this body of death? Thanks be to God—through Jesus Christ our Lord!" (Romans 7:25). We try to make it a point to pray with a time of confession and repentance before our worship services.

- **Self-consciousness and self-effort.** Both of these can cause us to worry about our performance. Self-effort keeps us on a treadmill where we seek to be "good and acceptable" by trying harder. Remember the Israelites and how they became emotionally and spiritually bound to "doing" good works? When we "try" to be acceptable to God and others, we end up feeling exhausted and burned out. The bottom line is this: We already are acceptable to God. He loves us. However, if we are only focused on our efforts and abilities, we will never come to a point where we experience His love and begin to build an intimate relationship with the Savior.

True worship comes when we learn to close our eyes and focus only on Him. We can stand unashamed in His glorious presence and sense His warmth and abiding love. In *The Practice of the Presence of God*, Brother Lawrence writes, "Pure love of Him is all that keeps me going." Pure love for our Savior is all that we need to sing a song of endless praise to His name.

*You can overcome self-consciousness and self-effort.* When I was very young, my father was not around much. However, when I started playing the guitar and performing, he began to show a great deal of interest in me. Some friends and I had formed a band, and my dad got bookings for us. He also made a point to show up for our rehearsals and come to every performance. While I appreciated the incredible attention my father gave me and the investment he made in my music career, it fed the thought that I will get attention and love when I perform.

Without knowing it when I grew up, I transferred this thought to my heavenly Father. I had a more difficult time connecting with God and others when I wasn't helping people, performing or leading worship. I thought I just was not as desirable to be around unless I was doing something that God or people valued. Now, I realize that God is not just interested in me when I minister or lead worship, but He desires to be with me because I am His son and He loves me.

The Bible tells us to fix our eyes on Jesus. (Hebrews 12:2) A change in focus is the best cure for self-consciousness and self-effort. Imagine trying to drive a car without looking at the road in front of you. If your eyes are focused on yourself, you will get off track; but if they are set on Jesus, you will stay perfectly on course.

Am I faced with the same temptations that others face? Yes! I have to constantly remind myself not to get caught up in the trappings of self by thinking how well I am doing as a pastor or worship leader. The purpose of worship leading is not to get attention by performing, but to lead others to a point where they lift their hearts, minds, and voice to God in adoration and praise. I have learned to rest in the fact that my relationship with God is not built on what I do but on what He already has done for me on the Cross.

• **Fear.** Fear robs us of the faith we need to come boldly before the throne of God. It distracts us and prevents us from worshiping and praising God. Fear has separated us from God since the first conversation after the fall when God said, "Adam, where art thou?" Adam answered, "I was afraid because I was naked; so I hid" (Genesis 3:10).

There is a story about how older lions in Africa catch their prey. Many cannot run as quickly as they did in their youth. However, their growl is just as fierce. They stalk their victims at night when it can't be seen that their growl is worse than their bite. Their prey hears them and becomes paralyzed with fear; then the lions can close in for the kill. The same is true of fear's growl. But we do not have to yield to fear's toothless roar. We have a mighty Savior, who is not afraid and stands at our side. In fact, as believers, He lives within us.

> We do not have to yield to fear's toothless roar. We have a mighty Savior, who is not afraid and stands at our side.

There is no need to fear because God is our everlasting strength, sovereign shield, infinite refuge, and eternal Savior. (Psalm 18)

*You can overcome the paralyzing effect of fear.* Because of God's great love and care for us, we really do not have a reason to be frightened. However, many Christians deal with thoughts of fear every day. Jesus understands those feelings, and He wants to teach us how overcome them.

He knew that once He was crucified, His disciples would be faced with a tremendous sense of fear. Therefore, after the resurrection, He appeared to them many times and told them to not be afraid. (John20:19) If you are struggling with feelings of fear, make a commitment to trust the One who holds your life securely in His hands. He will not let you go but will bring you through every difficulty. Jesus tells us, "In the world you have tribulation, but take courage; I have overcome the world" (John 16:33). Courage isn't the absence of fear. In fact, without something to be afraid of there is no need for courage. Courage is acting in faith despite your feelings of fear.

Once we learn that even the most courageous person feels

fear, we can take heart and press through the fear into a complete honesty and transparency that allows us to worship freely.

From time to time, I hear people saying how they long to experience the presence of God, but they are afraid of "coming" that close to Him. Perhaps, there is something in their past or their present that has them reluctant to opening their hearts up to the Lord. We do not ever have to be afraid of intimacy with God. The Israelites were, but they were living life under the Law. We are living under the covering of God's unconditional grace.

The apostle Paul reminded Timothy that God did not give us a spirit of timidity (or fear), but a spirit of power, of love and of self-discipline" (2 Timothy 1:7). This is His same reminder to us today.

For the times that we feel fearful, God wants us to know that perfect love—His love—drives out fear because fear has to do with punishment, and on the Cross, Jesus took our punishment for us. John writes, "God is love. Whoever lives in love lives in God, and God in him. In this way, love is made complete among us so that we will have confidence on the Day of Judgment, because in this world we are like him. There is no fear in love. But perfect love drives out fear, because fear has to do with punishment" (1 John 4:16b-18).

• **Selfishness.** When we want God to bless us and give us all that we want but are not willing to yield ourselves to Him, we have crossed a line and entered into selfishness. Throughout His Word, God tells us that we must not have any other gods before Him in our lives. Anything that would seek to take the place of the Savior is a barrier to our worship and faith in Christ. (Deuteronomy 5:7)

*You can overcome selfishness.* Worship is not just what we do with our lips; it is what we do with our lives. John Wimber, pastor, songwriter, and founder of the Vineyard movement, reminded us that "worship is the act of freely giving love to God—every activity of the Christian's life. If we only are focused on our-selves—our activities, needs, and desires then God will quickly be crowded out of our lives." Instead of continually pursuing God, we start to coast on our past momentum. The problem is that you can only coast when you're going downhill. And we may not recognize it till we crash at the bottom of our own self-absorption.

Esau was so interested in his personal needs being satisfied that he sold his birthright to his brother for a bowl of stew! He was the first-born in his family and would have received a wonder-ful inheritance had he not centered his focus on himself. (Genesis 25:29-34) As a result of his selfish behavior, he lost everything, and Jacob, who later became Israel, gained it all. But each of us has a wonderful inheritance, and we don't have to lose any por-tion of it.

Jesus Christ died for our sins and because of His great sacrifi-cial love, we can turn away from selfishness. Therefore, ask God to do the following:

• *Give you a clear understanding of what He personally has done for you.* When we realize all that God has saved us from, we will respond to Him in humility. He has protected our lives through dark and stormy times. He also has provided for every need we have.

• *Set your focus only on Him.* The author of Hebrews tells us to fix our eyes on Jesus. (Hebrews 12:2) When we do this, our hearts will be changed, we will reflect His love and we will be free to worship and praise God.

• *Remove areas of selfishness in your life.* Are there areas where you hold back from giving yourself out of an inordinate desire for comfort, your own way or preferences, fear, stinginess, envy or jealousy, pride or insecurity? We must remind ourselves, "What kind of deal is it to get everything you want but lose your own soul?" and "If you try to keep your life for yourself, you will lose it. But if you give up your life for my sake and for the sake of the Good News, you will find true life." (Matthew 16:26, The Message; Mark 8:35, NLT)

• *Get your eyes off yourself and on others.* Take time to get involved with other people. People are hurting all around us, and each one longs to hear about the love of God. You can be a bridge of hope to someone today, if you will lay aside all thoughts of selfishness and ask God to use you.

One of my top prayers has been a very dangerous one: "Lord, cleanse me from all earthly ambition and fill me with godly ambition." When I pray this prayer, usually two things happen. First, I find myself challenged about desires and motives for my ambitions. I start feeling nudges from the Holy Spirit asking why I am doing what I am doing. Is it for God's glory or mine? Second, I find myself challenged about why I am shrinking back from the ambitions and opportunities that God has given me. Am I afraid, too selfish to give what it takes? Or am I just more comfortable with being comfortable? Am I willing to look away from myself and look to God at all times?

Darlene Zschech reminds us that "worship is more than singing beautiful songs in church on Sunday. It is more than instruments and music. As a true Worshiper, your heart will long to worship Him at all times, in all ways, and with all your life." My prayer is that these words will be the deepest desire of your heart. Don't allow another moment to go by without asking God to tear away any veil that separates you from Him. Jesus tore down every barrier that keeps you from God. If you have never accepted His provision for eternal life, for unbroken relationship with God and for forgiveness of sins, you can do that right now by making Him Lord of your life. With Jesus as your Savior, you can receive the power of His grace to overcome any barrier to a life of intimate love and worship of God.

*Thank You, Jesus, that You came to earth to die for my sins. I ask that you would forgive me for each one. I also confess my need of You as Savior and Lord. I know that I cannot save myself. This is a gift that comes only from You through Your wondrous grace. Come into my life, Lord Jesus, and change me so that I will become a person of worship and praise and prayer. Amen*

## Chapter Four

# Let the Wind Blow

### flowing with the breath of God's spirit

*This is the air I breathe*
*This is the air I breathe*
*Your Holy Presence*
*Living in me.*

MARIE BARNETTE, "BREATHE"

While traveling in Florence, Italy, my wife and I would enter the museum and look at the great works of art, like Michelangelo's sculpture of David—and find ourselves breathing it all in. Years later in Israel, I saw a small manger near Bethlehem. The manger wasn't wooden like we commonly see it depicted but was a simple stone trough sculpted out of limestone. These two sculptures couldn't be further apart in appearance and artistry, yet they had a common effect on us; they were both greatly inspiring. The ways we worship may be as far apart as Michelangelo's David and a Bethlehem manger, but God's intent is that regardless of form, our worship should be inspiring and inspired. The word "inspire" literally means *to breathe in*. Meanings for the Hebrew and Greek words for "spirit" mean *breath* or *wind*. Just as with Adam when God "breathed into his nostrils the breath or spirit of life, and man became a living being" (Genesis 2:7, AMP), our worship and our lives come alive when they are inspired, filled with the breath of God's Spirit.

*To inspire* means:

- to influence, move, or guide by the Divine
- to exert an animating, enlivening, or exalting influence on
- to spur on, motivate, affect
- to breathe or blow into or upon
- to infuse (as life) by breathing

As we allow God's Spirit to breathe on us, we realize that worship is a response to His guiding, infusing, enlivening and motivating character and presence. In light of an all-inspiring God , worship is our response to who God is, what He has done in the past as well as what He's doing now.

When the prophet Isaiah saw the glory of the Lord in the temple, he was struck with the awesome reality of God's holiness and his own sinfulness. He was so overwhelmed by the inspiring presence of the Lord, that he:

1) Recognized the height of the awesome perfection and holiness of God and

2) Recognized the depth of his own sin that kept him from the only appropriate response to God's presence which is to worship him, offering himself to the Lord.

Since it is God's desire to be worshiped, He supplied the cleansing for Isaiah's sins to free him from everything that hindered that worship. He did this by touching Isaiah's "unclean lips" with a purifying fire of a coal from the altar. In the tabernacle, the place of worship for the Israelites, blood from the offering was poured out around the base of the altar. This foreshadowed the blood of Christ, the sacrificial lamb, flowing out when His side was pierced as He offered Himself for us on the cross.

When we are hindered from worship by our sin, Christ is able to purify us through the fire of his cleansing blood. Isaiah writes:

> I saw the Lord seated on a throne, high and exalted, and the train of his robe filled the temple. Above him were seraphs (fiery angelic worshiping beings) . . . And they were calling to one another: "Holy, holy, holy is the Lord Almighty; the whole earth is full of his glory."
>
> At the sound of their voices the doorposts and thresholds shook and the temple was filled with smoke.
>
> "Woe to me!" I cried. "I am ruined! For I am a man of unclean lips, and I live among a people of unclean lips, and my eyes have seen the King, the Lord Almighty."
>
> Then one of the seraphs flew to me with a live coal in his hand, which he had taken with tongs from the altar. With it he touched my mouth and said, "See, this has touched your lips; your guilt is taken away and your sin atoned for."
>
> — Isaiah 6:1-7

In this heavenly worship environment, Isaiah was responsive to the glory of God's presence. This led to confession, repentance and cleansing from his sins. He then offered himself with complete surrender as an act of worship (Romans 12) leading to his commissioning as a prophet of God. As we worship with sensitivity to the Spirit of the Lord, God's glory will fill us, "the temple of the living God" (2 Corinthians 6:16) and we will be empowered to fulfill whatever He calls us to. As a worship leader, my prayer has been to stay in tune with God's Spirit and not to do anything that would detract from the worship of Jesus Christ. Many times, it would be easy to manipulate the congregation's response through music. However, I don't believe this honors God or the people I am leading. We should not become loud or excited at a certain part in a song just because the song is usually sung that way. There may be times when we sing a song that way because the Spirit leads in that direction. However, there are other times, when we need to be soft and quiet. A worship leader's responsibility is to discern what the Holy Spirit is doing and present the songs in a way that is in tune with what the Spirit wants to accomplish at that moment.

During a succession of Sunday worship services, the leadership team at my church sensed the presence and transforming power of God at work in our congregation in a particularly strong way. Anticipating a "moving of the Spirit," we mentally and emotionally geared up for what we thought would come next as people surrendered their lives to Christ. However, God had something else in mind. Instead of ending in celebrative expression, our worship services began to end in quiet contemplation and consistent stillness. By thinking that we needed to "gear up" in the song, we realized that we had placed God in a box. We had set our expectations a certain way, but He had another plan in mind.

We could have continued to "plow" through the worship time by continuing to sing the songs that we had chosen in preparation for what we thought God was going to do, but we didn't. Instead, we chose to be still in our hearts and listen for the Lord's still small voice, knowing that He would lead us to the proper place of worship.

God has an agenda set for every worship service. He also has one scheduled for our personal times of devotion, and if we will ask Him to make us sensitive to His will, He will do it. We also will experience a true blessing as He accomplishes His purposes in our lives. So, we refused to rush ahead of the Lord. We waited and resisted the temptation to make our songs big and majestic, especially since the Spirit was revealing Himself in a gentle reverent way. We allowed the Spirit to orchestrate the services by not manipulating the worship. We changed the songs we had scheduled by removing the ones that didn't fit with what God was doing in our church at that moment and by modifying the way we did other songs to represent what the Spirit was doing. We sensed the direction of God's Spirit by watching and listening to what He was doing in our own lives and the lives of others.

Following God's Spirit is very moving and rewarding, especially when we are not manufacturing worship but truly seeking to experience and enjoy an intimate relationship with Christ. Worship leader Darlene Zschech writes, "True worship is when your spirit adores and connects with the Spirit of God . . . when the very core of our being is found in loving Him and being lost in Him."

## DEVELOPING A SPIRIT OF WORSHIP

Michael Catt, Pastor of Sherwood Baptist Church in Albany, Ga., tells us, "If we are going to worship in Spirit, we must develop a spirit of worship." I believe that there are some very practical applications that enhance our ability to have Spirit-led times of praise and worship. In fact, if worship is not led by God's Spirit then it is not worship at all because as we have learned earlier: "God is spirit and His worshipers must worship in spirit and truth" (John 4:24).

Developing worship that is in tune with His Spirit requires our commitment to do the following:

• **Let go of our desire to do what we've always done or how we've always done it and follow what God is telling us to do presently.** It is so easy to get locked into a form to the point where we are following our habits or routine rather than following the Holy Spirit. We can also be so used to a style that we move right past an opportunity to change it or try something different that many be more in tune with what God's doing in a given worship time. Michael Catt also said, "We are not seeking a style, or a form, we are seeking the Lord." If we are willing to watch and listen to the winds and waves of the Holy Spirit, God will lead us into worship that aligns with Him and His purposes. I am by no means saying to avoid planning or to throw out your list every week. In fact, planning can help get you prepared so that you are free to take detours if God leads. If we have no map at all, we can end up just wandering around never getting anywhere. But if our map's goal is to get us to the destination of God's presence, we must be willing to take a detour if the original road is closed or follow a more direct route if someone who is familiar with the journey, namely the Holy Spirit, leads us down a different path.

• **Be willing to "depart from the chart."** Like our roadmap, charts can either lead us to where we want to go or prevent us from experiencing the most glorious scenic views of places that are just off the beaten path. If we always just stay to the exact arrangement, we can find ourselves merely following the chart instead of flowing with the Holy Spirit. While we were in Israel, we learned that the steps leading to the temple are of varied heights and widths. It sure would have been easier to negotiate had they all been the same, but the wise and insightful men who designed them didn't want people to mindlessly approach the place of God's presence. They wanted them to have to think about every step to consider what they were doing and why. It's the same with our dependence on form or arrangement. I am known as somewhat of a stickler when it comes to the learning the parts of a song we are rehearsing, but I will tell the team that we cannot be sure of the arrangement. This makes some worship team members uncomfortable, but I think it is better than making all of the steps so pre-determined that we don't have to think about what the real purpose is—to have a present encounter with God.

This, of course, is not a license to extend every song or the length of the musical worship time beyond what the pastor and church leadership has requested. Once a pastor sees that worship leaders can be flexible and follow the Spirit without taking time from the other parts of the service, they will often be open to occasionally allowing extra time to pursue a spontaneous flow as the Spirit moves.

• **Let go of personal expectations and enjoy being in God's presence.** There have been times when I have started leading a worship service in one direction and have sensed the Lord turning it in another. Had I stuck with my goals, I would have frustrated the plan that God had for that particular service. While I also had a plan and a purpose for worship, I continually pray to be open to the leading of His Spirit.

These are principles that we also can apply to our personal times of worship. Our quiet times need to have structure, but they also need to be influenced and shaped by the heart and Spirit of God. There may be days when all you want to do is pray and read His Word. Two days later, you may find that all you want to do is sing and praise God. There is one thing that you can be sure of: If you stay in tune with His Spirit and with His Word, you will grow spiritually and get closer to God through worship and prayer.

## PLAY THE SUNSET

In the movie "Mr. Holland's Opus," Mr. Holland, the music teacher is trying to get one of his students to "play beyond" the notes on the page. When the young woman didn't understand what he was asking her to do, he stopped and asked her what she liked about herself. The student smiled and immediately answered, "My red hair because my father says it reminds him of the sunset."

That was all the information that Mr. Holland needed to press his point. "Then play the sunset," he instructed her. As the student began to play her instrument, the music lifted from note to emote, from technical performance to an expression of beauty. When we worship past our form, performance and conformance, God reveals his beauty and His characteristics. As we "play the sunset" through worship and song, God reveals Himself to us, our lives are transformed, and we become people who tune into and manifest the Spirit in holiness, mercy, grace, glory, power, tenderness, peace, and love.

God's fingerprints are in all of creation, whether it is a sunset or the sensation of the wind blowing around us. When we gather to worship, something should stir us to sing and express our love for God in such a way that He is glorified and lifted up. Worship through music and song parallels God's work in His creation. It was not a stretch for Mr. Holland to say, "Play the sunset" because God created this along with the wind, the rain, the mountains, the seas, and everything else.

Edwin Hatch was a distinguished lecturer in ecclesiastical history at Oxford College in Quebec. He could put together sentences that were filled with multi-syllabic words of unlimited description. However, when it came to expressing his faith in Christ, he wrote out a simple, heart-felt prayer in the form an age-old hymn entitled "Breathe on Me":

> Holy Spirit, breathe on me,
> Until my heart is clean;
> Let sunshine fill its inmost part,
> With not a cloud between.

> Breathe on me, breathe on me,
> Holy Spirit, breathe on me;
> Take thou my heart, cleanse every part,
> Holy Spirit, breathe on me.

The Greek word for "spirit" is *pneuma*, which means *a current of air—a breath, blast, or breeze.* God showed up at Pentecost as a mighty "rushing wind." (Acts 2:2) Sometimes His Spirit blows around us like a gentle breeze. Other times it may feel more like a hurricane. Then it can turn soft like a whisper before becoming strong like thunder or a tornado. Elijah expected the Lord to speak to him through a violent storm, but instead, the word of the Lord came to the prophet in the form of a whisper. (1 Kings 19:11-13) God comes to us according to His purpose for the moment. You may find that He smiles with you. Other times, He weeps over the hurts you suffer. He can laugh but He also can be direct and "to the point."

God's glory and presence is not limited to or confined to humanity's ideals or to the way He has come to us in the past. We just cannot put Him in a box. This is why it is so important for us to be sensitive to His Spirit in times of worship.

At times, our worship may be the following:

**Loud.** In Psalm 150, the psalmist expresses his praise for God's greatness:

> Praise the Lord. Praise God in his sanctuary; praise him in his mighty heavens. Praise him for his acts of power; praise him for his surpassing greatness. Praise him with the sounding of the trumpet, praise him with the harp and lyre, praise him with tambourine and dancing, praise him with the strings and flute, praise him with the clash of cymbals, praise him with resounding cymbals. Let everything that has breath praise the Lord.
>
> — Psalm 150

The word "resounding" here means *loud, an alarm, signal, blast or war-cry.* Please don't make this an excuse to blast people out or to turn your sound tech completely loose, but sometimes worship should rock the house.

**Still.** There are times when all God wants us to do is to be still before Him. He says, "Be still and know that I am God; I will be exalted among the nations, I will be exalted in the earth" (Psalm 46:10). When God spoke to Elijah, it was in a "[sound of gentle stillness and] a still, small voice" (1 Kings 19:12, AMP). When God is speaking to people in our churches in a still, small voice, we need to play and sing in a way that sets an atmosphere where He can be heard.

**Quiet.** Most of the time, we are people of activity. Even in times of rest, we like to be doing something. We hope that God will make His presence known to us in our frenetic activity, but He often waits until we have exhausted resources and ourselves. Then He speaks to our hearts. One phase in the prophet Elijah's life demonstrates this perfectly. He was on the run from the revenge-driven, prophet-hating queen, Jezebel, who had vowed to kill him. He had just witnessed a major miracle as God slew the prophets of Baal on Mt. Carmel. However, he was in need of a word of encouragement from God. Instead of choosing to be still and steadfast in his faith, he ran for his life! Finally, he came to the end of himself and his emotions at Horeb, the mountain of God. It was there that Lord instructed Elijah:

> "Go out and stand on the mountain in the presence of the Lord, for the Lord is about to pass by." Then a great and powerful wind tore the mountains apart and shattered the rocks before the Lord, but the Lord was not in the wind. After wind there was an earthquake, but the Lord was not in the earthquake. After the earthquake came a fire, but the Lord was not in the fire. And after the fire came a gentle whisper.
>
> – 1 Kings 19:11-12

God waits for us to come to a point of utter surrender, and then He can speak knowing that we will hear His voice.

While on a men's retreat in Mexico, I broke my collarbone and fractured my arm while riding (actually falling off) an ATV. Aside from the X-ray machine that the nurse had to literally bang on with her fist to get working, the most frightening part for me was having to lie quietly on the couch for weeks. However, once I got past the initial dread, I found that God used that time to speak to me in ways that I would have missed had I continued my usual routine.

## RIDING THE WAVE OF THE SPIRIT

It is no coincidence that worship is expressed so powerfully through the dynamics of music. When we study the way the sound waves of music work together, we realize just how powerful our unity and alignment with the Holy Spirit can be. Just like with sound waves, when we "flow" with God's Spirit in worship—in alignment and in phase with what He is doing—our praise amplifies His purposes in our hearts and lives. However, when we are out of sync with the Spirit, we actually can diminish the power of God's presence in our worship.

When God speaks it creates waves in the Sprit.

When we are in phase, tracking with the Spirit, it amplifies the intensity and power.

When two sounds are 180% apart, they cancel each other out and the net effect is flat lined. If we are out of sync and fail to "keep in step with the spirit" we can diminish the impact of God's presence. Even though we may have been musically well prepared, if our hearts are not engaged and aligned with the Holy Spirit, our worship will become flat and meaningless.

## GETTING IN TUNE WITH GOD

During a particularly difficult worship set, the struggle to "break through" and welcome God's spirit into our service became almost unbearable. The band seemed to be "out of sync," the people were distracted, and the message of worship was just not getting across. As the third song painfully wound down to a soft close, the other instruments got softer until just the acoustic guitar remained strumming. A very dissonant sound emerged. Suddenly, I realized that the guitarist had forgotten to put their capo on and had played the entire song in the wrong key!

When we don't tune into what the Spirit is doing through worship, we might as well be playing in a different key. This can happen when the following occurs:

• **The congregation hasn't prepared to worship.** When people have not worshiped the Lord throughout the week, they become more "in tune" with their own problems and concerns. They are easily distracted and preoccupied with things other than God. Self-focus diminishes the unity of the Spirit and the ability to connect with the Lord in one voice. When this happens, it is helpful for the worship leader and team to press through with some "focus on God" moments and declarative songs that remind us of God's attributes and character.

• **The worship team is not focused on God but on performance, personal agendas, and the technical aspect of worship rather than on the Lord.** When we use our voices for purposes other than God's glory (our ego, need for popularity, attention or for just a fulfilling experience) then our worship becomes a bunch of Babylon babble. God resisted, scattered and confounded the language of the people in Babel (Babylon) because they used their abilities to make a name for and glorify themselves instead of God. "Come, let us build ourselves a city, with a tower that reaches to the heavens, so that we may make a name for ourselves" (Genesis 11:4). Contrast their pride with the true humility written about by Amy Carmichael: "If I cannot in honest happiness take the second place (or the twentieth); if I cannot take the first without making a fuss about my unworthiness, then I know nothing of Calvary love."

• **The worship team is not prepared for the service and ends up being worried about the music and how they sound instead of just worshiping and praising.** Attention to ourselves cancels out or diminishes the effectiveness and intensity of God's presence. Self consciousness undermines God consciousness. Our goal for worship should be just to be with God and nothing else. John Wimber writes, "What happens when we are alone with the Lord determines how intimate and deep the worship will be when we come together."

• **There are unresolved conflicts within the team, the leadership or the congregation.** If there are conflicts with others, our worship and praise will be blocked and stagnate. God tells us that we should even lay aside worship until our conflicts are addressed. (Matthew 5:23) He also tells us that we really can't genuinely worship Him if we aren't loving each other. (1 John 4:20)

•**We have thrown out the baby with the bathwater concerning worship expressions.** The New Age movement has borrowed the godly concepts of meditating and getting in tune with God. Adherents of this false religion mistakenly seek to be "in touch" with their inner being and spirit guides in an effort to multiply the power of God in their lives. However, they are deceived. They may be "worshiping" in spirit, but they are not worshiping the true Spirit—the Holy Spirit of God. And it certainly is not the truth. But, God designed us to meditate on His goodness, truth, and love. In fact, the Bible instructs us to meditate on the Word of God and to come before His throne with thanksgiving and song. (Psalm 95:2) In Hebrew, meditate means "to commune, speak, study, consider, ponder, or sing." The Psalms are filled with words that can stir our hearts to worship and to godly meditation as we consider His unfailing love (48:9), His works and mighty deeds (77:12), His precepts and ways (119:15), His wonders (119:27), and His promises (119:148).

## THE LEVITES GOT IT RIGHT

In 2 Chronicles we read that "all the Levites who were musicians ... stood ... playing cymbals, harps and lyres. They were accompanied by 120 priests sounding trumpets. The trumpeters and singers joined in unison, as with one voice, to give praise and thanks to the Lord. Accompanied by trumpets, cymbals and other instruments, they raised their voices in praise to the Lord and sang: He is good; his love endures forever. Then the temple of the Lord was filled with a cloud, and the priests could not perform their service because of the cloud, for the glory of the Lord filled the temple of God" (2 Chronicles 12-14).

This passage describes a sense of harmony and unity of spirit among the people. No one was trying to be out front and be noticed. Instead, they had prepared for and pursued the singular desire of glorifying God through their praise and worship. For us, this may mean sticking to a schedule that we have pulled together but other times it may mean being flexible so the Spirit can work through our worship.

At the end of a Sunday morning worship set, I started into the last song we had scheduled. About four bars in, I sensed that God's purposes for our time were completed during the previous song. So, I brought the worship team to an awkward halt by waving my hands and saying into the microphone, "Wait a minute, wait a minute, stop ... hold on!"

Then I explained to the congregation, "You know, we already have accomplished God's purposes for this worship time. We had this last song scheduled, but it has nothing to add to the significant move of the Spirit that we've had until this point. So let's not just do a song because it was on the list. Let's allow God to direct." The congregation applauded enthusiastically with senses that we were in God's presence and responding to the leading of the Spirit. Later, numerous people told me that it affected them greatly. It made them feel secure and valued because I was committed to following God and not trying to "hype" anything or musically manipulate people into responding to something other than the Spirit of God.

Often when people tell me that they had a wonderful experience in worship at our church in Atlanta, I tell them that our congregation is so eager and prepared to worship that leading them in praise is just like surfing. It is just a matter of recognizing the wave of the Spirit, watching the swell grow as they respond, catching the wave as it comes by, and letting it carry us along. I often feel like I'm not really leading or directing; I'm just along for the ride!

How are you responding to the wind and the waves of God's Spirit in worship? Are you just "rowing through the motions" or setting your sails to catch the wind of the Spirit and letting it take you wherever and however it blows?

*Lord, help me to worship in spirit and in truth. Make me sensitive to Your Spirit's voice so that I will follow Your lead as I offer myself to you in worship. Stir my spirit, soul and body to respond to the wind of your Spirit as I come before Your holy presence.*

*"... true worshipers will worship the Father in spirit and truth, for they are the kind of worshipers the Father seeks. God is spirit, and His worshipers must worship in spirit and in truth" (John 4:23-24).*

# Chapter Five

# "War"ship

## worshiping on the front lines

*The crowd joined in the attack against Paul and Silas,*
*and the magistrates ordered them to be stripped and beaten.*
*After they had been severely flogged, they were thrown into prison.*
*About midnight Paul and Silas were praying*
*And singing hymns to God, and the other*
*Prisoners were listening to them.*

ACTS 16:22-25

*Now order the ranks, and fling wide the banners,*
*for our souls are God's and our bodies the king's.*

SIR ARTHUR CONAN DOYLE, "THE WHITE COMPANY"

The first service for the Church that I pastor was scheduled for September 11, 2005. Little did we know that Hurricane Katrina would hit less than two weeks before. We produced a video of footage from the hurricane disaster and from the terrorist attacks of September 11, 2001, accompanied by the worship song, "Yet I will Praise." As the devastating images assaulted our minds, our hearts aligned with the words:

Even in the darkest valley,
I will praise You, Lord.
And when my world is shattered
And it seems all hope is gone,
Yet, I will praise You, Lord.

God calls us to not only praise Him from the mountain tops but in the deepest valleys, even the valley of the shadow of death.

In light of tragedies like September 11, 2001, the Indian Ocean Tsunami, and Hurricane Katrina, this may seem difficult if not impossible to do, but our faith requires that we praise Him when we are panicked, worship Him when we are whipped, and sing to Him when we are sinking.

David has given us one of the most stirring examples of praise in the midst of anguish in Psalm 23, written during one of the loneliest and most trying moments of his life:

The Lord is my shepherd; I shall not be in want. He makes me lie down in green pastures, He leads me beside quiet waters, He restores my soul. He guides me in paths of righteousness for his name's sake. Even though I walk through the valley of the shadow of death, I will fear no evil. . . . Surely goodness and love will follow me all the days of my life, and I will dwell in the house of the Lord forever.

– Psalms 23 1-4; 6

## FAITH TO ENDURE FOR SURE

David was destined to rule and be the model worshiper. Yet, before he could take hold of his destiny, he had much to learn. Early in his life, God placed him in a classroom of difficulty and loneliness. Often, David was left alone by his family to guard and protect the flock. As he chose to focus on God during this time, his courage and hope increased.

When a bear or a lion threatened to attack, David fought off the enemy. (1 Samuel 17:34-36) When fears closed in on him, he stood firm in his faith. (Psalm 18:1-6) It was in the sheep field that God shaped David's heart into one after His "own heart." (Acts 13:22) The Lord took his servant through this training to strengthen and prepare him to face a greater challenge to come— the life threatening giant, Goliath.

As our world has faced its own Goliaths during the man-made and natural disasters of recent years, praising God in the midst of terror and uncertainty lifts us, like it did David, from the present reality of the shaken earth to the eternal reality of the unshakable rock. It reinforces our belief that in spite of cataclysmic events, God can and will be glorified.

Adversity also offers us an opportunity to demonstrate whether our faith is made of gold or straw. As we learn to praise God in the midst of a terrible trial, we develop a sense of perseverance and consistent hope. James wrote to New Testament believers who were living in extreme circumstances. Through severe persecution, many had been forced to leave their homes and families. Yet, they endured and the testimony of Christ's life and death began to spread throughout the world. Underground churches were formed with worship and praise at the core of their existence. James admonished early believers to "consider it pure joy" when trouble comes. The writer of Hebrews tells us how, "We do this by keeping our eyes on Jesus, on whom our faith depends from start to finish" (Hebrews 12:2).

We may feel like we have a strong faith, but it is testing that proves it. When it comes to faith, there is no conquest without a contest—no triumph without a trial, no testimony without the test, and no gain without the pain. Even Jesus knew that He could not gain the crown without the Cross.

In *The Life and Works of the Reverend Charles H. Spurgeon,* he reminds us that, "The man who reckons that he can glide into heaven without a struggle has made a great mistake." The Bible is filled with examples of those who had to endure both trial and testing in order to become men and women of great faith and praise. So, if God is requiring you to endure great difficulty at this point in your life, at least you are in good company.

## WORSHIP BRINGS FREEDOM

In Acts 16, Paul and Silas traveled through Macedonia to preach the Word. At one point in their journey both men were severely beaten and then imprisoned: "About midnight Paul and Silas were praying and singing hymns to God, and the other prisoners were listening to them. Suddenly there was such a violent earthquake that the foundations of the prison were shaken. At once all the prison doors flew open, and everybody's chains came loose" (Acts 16:25-26).

Praise doesn't only bring freedom, it brings salvation. The jailer woke up and was sure that everyone had escaped and was about to kill himself, but Paul assured him by saying, "Don't harm yourself! We are all here!" (Acts 16:27-28). The jailer was so overcome with the power of the presence of God that he fell trembling before Paul and Silas and asked how he could be saved. The other prisoners came rushing forward and said, "We want the God you've got!" Everyone's eyes were opened wide to the earth-shaking, chain- breaking, miracle making God. All because of two imprisoned and severely beaten men who cried out to God in worship and prayer. Jesus tells us that when we lift Him up to others, He will draw all men and women to Himself" (John 12:32).

John Wimber writes, "We don't worship God in order to get blessed, but we are blessed as we worship him. He visits his people with manifestations of the Holy Spirit. He moves in different ways—sometimes for salvation, sometimes for deliverance, sometimes for sanctification or healing." Worship ushers us into the presence of God. It is God's presence that changes our circumstances—and changes us. In fact, the only thing that has the power to change our world is God. The atmosphere of worship draws people to God through His Holy Spirit. This is what happened the night that Paul and Silas began to sing.

Recently, a friend of mine, who leads worship at youth conferences throughout the U.S. told me that a youth approached him after a conference session saying that he had given his life to Jesus during the worship time. This happened before any message had been preached or any altar call had been given. The power and presence of God was so strong in worship that this young man responded to the Holy Spirit and became a believer right then.

The last time I was in Brazil, a woman came to me after our service. She told me that during my visit a year earlier she had had been crippled and unable to walk and was brought forward at the end of one of our worship conferences to receive prayer. I had prayed and asked God to heal her. As she now stood before me, I recognized that she had just walked up to me completely unhindered and was standing on her own two feet. She thanked me and praised God for the healing she had received. This time she had brought her daughter with her who was suffering from several diseases and wanted me to again pray. Explaining to her that it was not me, but God that healed her, I obliged and prayed for her daughter. I am convinced that the presence of God in worship created the healing atmosphere that empowered my prayers and fanned the flame of this woman's faith for the healing.

## WORSHIP BRINGS DELIVERANCE

As we worship God, the atmosphere of heaven invades our hearts and minds bringing with it deliverance. We also are freed from Satan's harassment as we focus on our desire for Jesus. There were times in King Saul's life when an evil spirit oppressed him. Most of us have felt the enemy's oppressive influence. What is amazing is that Saul knew enough to seek help through music and worship.

> Saul said to his attendants, "Find someone who plays well and bring him to me." One of the servants answered, "I have seen a son of Jesse of Bethlehem who knows how to play the harp ... And the Lord is with him."
>
> At Saul's request, David entered his service and, whenever the spirit from God came upon Saul, David would take his harp and play. Then relief would come to Saul; he would feel better, and the evil spirit would leave him.
>
> — 1 Samuel 16:16-21; 23

Reading these verses, we realize that when we worship the Lord the way David did—tapping into the clouds of heaven—it lifts the clouds of oppression away from us. The psalms that David wrote were much like the worship songs of today, poems that were sung accompanied by stringed instruments. Though we read them as prose and sometimes as poetry, it has been "proposed that those little marks above and below the lines (in the Hebrew Bible) are MUSICAL SCORES . . . indicating that much, apparently, if not all of the Old Testament was meant to be recited to music." (Newsletter of the Associates for Biblical Research, March 1982) David was an accomplished musician and knew the value of worshiping God to music. We know, of course, that eventually Saul didn't choose to follow the Lord with a whole heart. Ultimately God chose the worshiping servant, David, to replace the self-possessed Saul as King of Israel.

Some of the songs David played for Saul could have easily been the ones he penned in the book of Psalms. Just imagine the effect it had on Saul as he listened to this song that David wrote:

> The Lord is my shepherd, I shall not be in want.
> He makes me lie down in green pastures,
> he leads me beside quiet waters,
> he restores my soul.
> He guides me in paths of righteousness
> for his name's sake.
> Even though I walk
> through the valley of the shadow of death,
> I will fear no evil,
> for you are with me.
>
> – Psalm 23:1-4

Saul probably thought he faced death as he walked in utter fear from the torment of the evil spirit. He certainly would have lacked the peace, calm and quiet assurance that David brought with these passages. Like Saul being delivered through David's Psalms, I have seen people experience remarkable release from oppression as we have sung Scott Underwood's song, "You Are in Control":

> You are my shepherd, I have no needs
> You lead me by peaceful streams
> And You refresh my life
>
> You hold my hand and You guide my steps
> I could walk through the valley of death
> And I won't be afraid
> Because You are in control

David was a great psalmist because he discovered first hand what it was like to find comfort and deliverance in the worship of

God as evidenced in Psalm 32. This worship song is David's grateful testimony to God's forgiveness, mercy and grace in his own life. He had sinned against God and needed deliverance from sin, which the Lord always provides when we ask. In his joy and relief he penned these words, "Therefore let everyone who is godly pray to you while you may be found; surely when the mighty waters rise, they will not reach him. You are my hiding place; you will protect me from trouble and surround me with songs of deliverance" (Psalm 32:6-7). We often think of worship merely as songs we sing to God, but God actually surrounds us with His songs of deliverance as we worship Him.

## THE FREEDOM TRAIN

Historians tell about the songs the slaves sang in their captivity before the American Civil War. In taking a closer look at these songs, we find not only the musical and emotional elements that inspired blues, rock, jazz and R&B, but also a heart cry for helping others toward freedom and deliverance. They had titles like "Near the Lake Where Drooped the Willow," "Wade in the Water," and "Follow the Drinking Gourd."

Picture people, not unlike the people of Israel who were enslaved in Egypt, desperate for freedom and crying out for deliverance as you read the lyrics from "Follow the Drinking Gourd."

When the sun comes up and the first quail calls,
follow the drinking gourd.
For the old man is a-waiting to carry you to freedom,
If you follow the drinking gourd.

The river ends between two hills.
Follow the drinking gourd.
There's another river on the other side,

Follow the drinking gourd.

Where the great big river meets the little river,
Follow the drinking gourd.
For the old man is a-waiting for to carry you to freedom
If you follow the drinking gourd.

Slave songs like this one not only provided vivid imagery, they pointed to literal landmarks and directions to get to the "Underground Railway" that would transport escaped slaves to freedom. In this song "Follow the Drinking Gourd," the "drinking gourd" is the big dipper, which pointed to the north and safe houses. As they sang this song, it would tell other slaves to get up at sunrise, look for the big dipper and follow it north past two mountains to a man stationed at the fork where a large and small river meet. This man would then get them aboard the "Underground Railroad" which would take them to safe houses set up for escaped slaves.

When we sing worship songs, we are telling each other to arise and look up to Jesus who will lead us to God, carrying us past the mountains of our trials along the flowing river of His spirit. Worship songs are songs of freedom that point to the safe house of God's dwelling place, His presence. Worship carries us out of enslavement to our present circumstances and far from the torment of the enemy, our former master.

Slaves were often forbidden to have conversations with one another so they sang these songs of deliverance. When problems increase, or when trouble strikes without warning and no words will convey our fears or anguish, worship can become the compass pointing the way to deliverance and eternal hope.

Jesus is our eternal hope. He is the only One who can bring us to the point of freedom. When we follow His star, we board a freedom train that leads us to the throne room of God where the

Father welcomes us to His place of eternal safety. In a song that David wrote, the lyrics say, "For in the day of trouble he will keep me safe in his dwelling; he will hide me in the shelter of his tabernacle and set me high upon a rock" (Psalm 27:5). Whether we face the danger of lions or bears as David did, or just the troubles of the "jungle out there," we can get to freedom through the deliverance that worship brings.

The songs the slaves once sang led to the writing of many of the gospel songs that emerged in the following decades. These songs were more often about heaven and "the sweet bye and bye" than they were about earthly freedom. The slave songs of physical freedom lead to the creation of songs of spiritual freedom. They reveal the hope, power, and ingenuity of an enslaved people, who used their traditions, passions, and resources to express their faith. Through our worship of God, we can do the same thing. Is it any wonder that these "songs of deliverance" served as the blueprint to so many spirituals for the last 150 years?

## JUST GET ON BOARD

People get ready, there's a train a comin'
You don't need no baggage, you just get on board
All you need is faith to hear the diesels hummin'
You don't need no ticket you just thank the Lord
— Curtis Mayfield, "People Get Ready"

One day, I kept feeling that I was supposed to lead worship for one of our Alpha meetings, an introductory course to Christianity. This is not something I regularly do, but I couldn't shake the nagging feeling that I was supposed to be there. At the end of the set for Alpha, I expected to pray briefly and then invite the people to sit down for the presentation, but God had other plans. As the last song came to a close, there was an overwhelming sense of God's presence in the room. Everyone stood in complete silence for minutes. God was clearly revealing His glory to us. As we stood there soaking in God's presence, one young woman seemed completely enveloped by the Lord. I knew that she was new to our church and I was moved to see her so deeply engaged in worship. She later told me that although she grew up in church, she had walked away from religion and had only recently become a Christian. She said that what she experienced in worship was what transformed her life.

Worship has the ability to usher us into God's presence like nothing else. There is something about being with Him that is irresistible. In times of worship, He reveals Himself to us and draws us near to His never-ending fountain of mercy and love. When we worship Him, it transcends our natural thoughts and senses and the circumstances of life—worries, fears, and human aspirations quickly fall away because we are connected with the eternal, almighty God, who is also our loving heavenly Father.

When God's people use the musical talents, instruments, and voices that He has given them for His glory, then the power of His presence will fall upon the people who are worshiping Him. Something happens when we join together and set aside time to worship Him. His presence in our corporate worship confirms that wherever two or more are gathered together in His name, He is there among them.

The psalmist writes in Psalm 84: "Better is one day in your courts than a thousand elsewhere; I would rather be a doorkeeper in the house of my God than dwell in the tents of the wicked" (vs. 10). Coming to God's "house" is not about just coming to a church building. We are the building, we are the church. 1 Corinthians 3:16 tells us, "You realize, don't you, that you are the temple of God, and God himself is present in you?" (The Message).

God is still saying the same thing to us today as he said to His people in Exodus 25:8, "Then have them make a sanctuary for me and I will dwell among them." God is asking us to prepare our hearts as a sanctuary so that He can dwell there. God is telling us to corporately and individually build ourselves into a place that He will inhabit. We want to be a temple He doesn't just occasionally visit, but one where He actually resides. Worship creates that place in and among us because God inhabits the praise of His people. (Psalm 22:3)

When we sing Casey Corum's song "Dwell", we are aligning with God's desires as we sing:

> Dwell in the midst of us
> come and dwell in this place
> dwell in the midst of us
> Lord you can have your own way.

Let that be our heart cry, as we gather together in worship, "being built together to become a dwelling in which God lives by his spirit" (Ephesians 2:22). This verse speaks of the unity we have if we will join together in worship. Without praising and living in unity, our worship and our witness are discordant and empty. But as we worship with one heart and one mind, we'll find God living among us and filling us with His treasures. These are the kind of Worshipers about whom God says, "They will be my people, and I will be their God. And I will give them one heart and mind to worship me forever, for their own good and for the good of all their descendants. And I will make an everlasting covenant with them, promising not to stop doing good for them. I will put a desire in their hearts to worship me, and they will never leave me." (Jeremiah 32:38-40, NLT)

*Lord, increase the desire in my heart to worship you. Thank You that any battle that rages around me belongs to You. It is not mine to handle. Therefore, I will set my eyes on You and watch for your deliverance. Let all those who take refuge and put their trust in You rejoice; let them ever sing and shout for joy, because You make a covering over them and defend them. (Psalm 5:11, AMP)*

# Chapter Six

# Cry about the Battle or Sound the Battle Cry
## finding strength in worship

*The LORD himself will fight for you.*
*You won't have to lift a finger in your defense!.*

EXODUS 14:14, NLT

*But this is all I want,*
*It's all I need.*
*This is all I am,*
*It's everything . . .*
*Beat a drum for me*

R.E.M., "BANG A DRUM FOR ME"

While visiting Scotland, Trace and I were fascinated by a sign that was part of an exhibit in the Royal Scots Regimental Museum at the Edinburgh Castle. It read, "Drums were essential to the successful operation of the army as signaling instruments which sounded the 'Calls' telling the soldiers what to do in battle and in camp." When it comes to us, the army of God, our worship music, drums and all, sound the call for people to fight the good fight.

I have taught often about worshiping in the midst of life's battles. Personally, 2004 was my year to be sent to the front lines for some real life application of what I've taught. The end of the year was a particularly difficult season. My father had been in and out of the hospital for months. Faced with declining health, he now also had to face leaving his home of 50 years and move in with my sister who lived in another state. At the same time my responsibilities at church were undergoing major changes.

Just when I thought I couldn't handle any more, someone brazenly walked into our church and walked out with my new notebook computer, my acoustic guitar, cell phone, and my iPod. To make matters worse, my remaining computers at home all got viruses, my wife needed surgery, and my other cell phone stopped working. All of this took place in a matter of weeks, and the majority of it took place while I was producing a full-blown musical for Christmas at church. My father actually passed away right before our heaviest week of rehearsals. While planning a funeral and overseeing dozens of our worship arts volunteers, I found myself disoriented and heading toward burnout. I was amazed at how dependent I was on my gadgets and how susceptible I was to not being able to focus on God when things were tough. I found myself faced with the choice to either cry over the battle or sound the battle cry. Determined not to feel sorry for myself (though I sometimes did), I voiced a battle cry, though it was more of a whisper or a whimper than a victory shout. Weak as it was, I started praising God even when I didn't feel like it. I purposed to thank the Lord for what I knew ... that He is good and He is strong. Though it was a season when I didn't feel like

> I found myself faced with the choice to either cry over the battle or sound the battle cry.

delving into the Word, I held on to scriptures like, "When the enemy comes in like a flood, the spirit of the Lord will raise up a standard against him," (Isaiah 59:19, NASB) and "For we know that in all things, God works for the good of those who love Him" (Romans 8:28). I also determined to worship Him with a thankful attitude. I found out firsthand that stepping out in faith and worshiping God is not only an act of obedience, it actually changes us.

Through this ordeal, I started seeing situations and people differently. It helped me to see God's perspective on things and look for the fruit He would bring forth from my situations. When all of my things were taken, I called the cell phone that was stolen and left a message saying, "If you are the person who stole my stuff, you had better return it or you'll loose your blessing." OK, it was really corny, I'll admit it, but it was worth it to recall the astonished face of the other worship leader, whose guitar and laptop were also stolen, as he overheard me leaving the message. He told me later that it convicted him of the need to release the anger and to forgive whoever stole our stuff. Taking the high road of forgiveness was just one of the results of choosing to praise God in these challenging circumstances instead of just muddling my way through feeling overwhelmed and discouraged.

## PRAISE AND STAY PUT

It's not that my worship was "in the pocket" during these struggles like it is when life is running on all cylinders. For much of this season, I just ended up echoing the songwriter who penned the following words, "Why am I discouraged? Why so sad? I will put my hope in God! I will praise him again – my Savior and my God!" (Psalms 42:11, NLT).

The morning before my computer and gear were stolen, I seemed to be negotiating the rough circumstances I was going through fairly well and wasn't feeling particularly overwhelmed. I was at the church leading worship, meeting with our computer team and having lunch with some friends. This was pretty much the scenario for the people of Judah during King Jehoshaphat's reign. They didn't have computers or iPods that could be stolen, but the people of Jerusalem, like I was, were going about their normal tasks without contemplating the fact that an enemy was just over the horizon preparing to attack them. In 2 Chronicles, we find that the Moabites and the Amonites joined forces and declared war on God's people. Often when trouble comes our way we wonder why it has happened to us and agonize over what to do about it. Instead of wondering, speculating, and rushing around in a panic, the Bible says that Jehoshaphat "resolved to inquire of the Lord." The king didn't throw his arms up in fear or defeat. Instead, he turned to God through worship. He fell on his face before the Lord in prayer and then proclaimed a fast and the "people of Judah came together to seek help from the Lord" (2 Chronicles 20:1-4).

You can read Jehoshaphat's entire prayer in 2 Chronicles 20. Notice how this portion emphasizes the will and determination of the king. "If calamity comes upon us, whether the sword of judgment, or plague or famine, we will stand in your presence before this temple that bears your Name and will cry out to you in our distress, and you will hear us and save us" (v. 9). I want to have that kind of faith and confidence in God that says, "No matter what happens, I will cry out to You and You will rescue me."

Shortly after takeoff on a flight that my wife, Trace, and I were on, we heard a loud explosion. But, as the flight continued we realized that we were not gaining any altitude and that something was dreadfully wrong. As the plane shook and strained to stay aloft, we held hands, sang and prayed, "Lord, protect us and place your angels on the wings, but if this is our time, we entrust ourselves to You." We had lost an engine on take off, but the pilot was able to gain control and get us back to the airport safely. After we landed, the noticeably shaken pilot, his face an ashen gray, stood in the cockpit door telling us that had the engine exploded seconds earlier, we would have plummeted into the ground. Trace and I were astonished that throughout the ordeal we were able to act out our faith with such peace from God considering we were seconds from disaster. We had felt confident that our lives were in God's hands regardless of the outcome.

## "LET'S SEND THE WORSHIP TEAM OUT FRONT"

When King Jehoshaphat cried out to the Lord, God answered through the prophet Jaheziel with this: "Do not be afraid or discouraged because of this vast army. For the battle is not yours, but God's. Tomorrow march down against them. . . . You will not have to fight this battle. Take up your positions; stand firm and see the deliverance the Lord will give you, O Judah and Jerusalem. Do not be afraid; do not be discouraged. Go out to face them tomorrow, and the Lord will be with you" (2 Chronicles 20:15-17).

Once the people of Judah heard these words, they fell down in worship and sang one more song even though it was not on the "set list." Their hearts were totally turned to the Lord in praise. The next morning Judah's army prepared for battle. I can imagine them saying, "Now how's this gonna work? We get ready to fight, our enemy's getting ready to fight, but God says we won't have to." But, the people of Judah also knew the stories of their ancestors. True to His word, God fulfilled miraculous promises and granted miraculous victories to Abraham, Joseph, Moses, and David as they obeyed. So, their only responsibility was to stand on God's Word and trust Him for the victory.

"Early the next morning they left for the Desert of Tekoa. As they set out, Jehoshaphat stood and said, "Listen to me, Judah and the people of Jerusalem! Have faith in the Lord your God and you will be upheld; have faith in his prophets and you will be successful" (v. 20). There is a reason God instructs us to wait, believe His word and trust Him. He knows that if the focus of our hearts is set on the Word, Jesus, we will not become afraid in the midst of the battle. God wants each one of us to learn how to be courageous, strong in our faith, patient, and longsuffering. Many times in order for this to happen, we have to be willing to march into battle trusting only in the Lord and not in ourselves. Faith means that we see God as being in control of our circumstances, and consequently, we surrender to His plan. This was the position that Jehoshaphat took. He trusted and praised God for His coming deliverance. Then in faith, he decided on a strategy to place Judah's worship team in front of the entire army. This means that the guys with the "real weapons" were told to follow at a distant second. As a worship leader, that's not exactly the way I would have our tech team set up the stage.

> If the focus of our hearts is set on the Word, Jesus, we will not become afraid in the midst of the battle.

As a musician, I once did a USO tour, so I can imagine a little of what the scene could have been like. It would be like taking a team of musicians to Iraq. I could see us singing for the troops, providing moral support, maybe even leading a worship service, when the base commander tells us that a group of terrorists has blown up a nearby town and is heading for the base with fully armed soldiers. As thoughts race through my head of running for cover or figuring out a way for the musicians to escape fast, the sergeant informs me that we are holding a worship service with me up front, on the stage. I reluctantly call the team together trusting that the "military" and political leaders know how much time we have and what is important. During the service, the chaplain brings a prophetic word that "God is giving us this victory" and we will not have to fight. I sigh in relief expecting that some elite troops are going to stop the terrorists or that the head of the organization is miraculously caught. Just then the President of the U.S. calls and says God told him that we were supposed to send the musicians out to march in front of the army. The protests arise: "We don't even know how to work the guns!" The sergeant says, "You won't need guns; you're gonna sing us to victory." As a worship leader, I'm not sure I would have volunteered for this duty. But, when we join God's army we are worshiping on the front lines, affronting the enemy, equipped with praise and weapons of worship as we see God's victory unfold through His power manifesting where He is proclaimed and glorified.

Judah marched into battle that day singing, "Give thanks to the Lord, for his love endures forever." In our worship services when we sing Michael W. Smith's song "Forever"—"Give thanks to the Lord, for He is good, His love endures forever ... forever God is faithful, forever God is strong, forever God is with us ... Forever!"—we are singing the same victory song that the people of Judah did.

As the people sang praises to the Lord, God set ambushes among Judah's enemies and all who had risen up to fight against His people started fighting amongst themselves and destroyed each other. This is what happens in our lives. When the enemy assaults us, if we will praise God with weapons of worship, it will undermine the attack of our adversaries and lead us to victory.

Through the story of the people of Judah, God is showing us how to respond to the enemies that threaten us today. The tribes that attacked Judah represent the same things that attack us today. "Ammon" means *to overshadow*. Today unrighteousness threatens to overshadowed righteousness. "Ammon" also means *to become dim*. Paul exhorts us to "Live no longer as the ungodly do, for they are hopelessly confused. Their closed minds are full of darkness; they are far away from the life of God because they have shut their minds and hardened their hearts against him" (Ephesians 4:17-18)

Moab was an incestuous son of Lot. The Moabites represented the most hideous carnality—given over to total depravity and immorality. One night in front of prime time television or an hour of the news will confirm that immorality and our obsession with it have permeated our culture.

The word "seir" means *to be (horribly) afraid*. The instability of our world along with our cultural obsession with murder shows, crime exposes, and the demonic (myriad TV shows and movies), have caused fear to be endemic in our society. When I talk to believers, the most prevalent issue they have is fear. This is not coincidence because:

- Fear is the number one tool of the enemy
- The enemy can smell fear a mile away

"Jehoshaphat" means *the Lord has judged*. Just like the people of Judah and Jerusalem, we are in a time of the Lord's judgment. The Lord is still telling His people to "stand still and be at peace in the midst of the storm. This is my battle. I will fight it. You don't have to. The battle is too great for you, but I will bring the victory over this darkness if you will worship, pray, and obey." "Judah" means *to hold out the hand; especially to revere or worship with extended hands with thanksgiving*. This is the people of worship God is calling us to be.

When we sing praises, we bring people out of the shadows of unrighteousness, immorality, fear, and sin. We'll talk more about fear later, but we need to know that praise and worship reminds Satan that even with his fear tactics, the victory always belongs to the Lord. Before his fall, Lucifer's ministry in heaven was to lead the worship. His name means "light," and his primary responsibility was to offer praise and worship to magnify the illuminating glory of God. When we worship Christ, we remind "Lucifer," now the prince of darkness, of what he has given up and how far he has fallen. To him and his hoard, our words of worship are like fingernails raked across a chalkboard.

## GETTING A FAITH LIFT

When faced with terrifying news, Jehoshaphat could have said, "I'm going to consult my military leaders and muster up all the resources we have and fight with all our strength." He also could have called the people together and told them to "run for their lives." Instead, he stood firm in his faith in God's power and strength. He knew the sovereign Lord of heaven was aware of Judah's circumstances and would bring deliverance.

God may allow you to be tested in the heat of battle in order to reveal your level of faith, but He will never abandon you. If your hope and faith is set on Him, He will bring you through the valley victoriously.

What can we learn from the story of Judah's deliverance from its enemies?

• **When faced with insurmountable opposition, turn to God first.** Our tendency is to try everything imaginable in order to be rescued. Finally, when we have used up all our options and we are totally exhausted, we turn to God for help. However, our first choice needs to be to turn to Him through prayer and worship.

• **Fast.** Fasting focuses our minds on the Lord and provides an opportunity for Him to speak to our hearts. If you cannot fast from food for health reasons, ask the Lord to show you something else you can give up for a season as an act of devotion and preparation for blessing.

• **Pray.** Prayer to God is one of the most powerful weapons we have. It is our communication with a holy, righteous God and it never fails to usher us into His throne room of acceptance and hope. When we pray, God listens. His heart is turned toward us and He is moved by our words of faith and praise. Be sure when you pray that you are praying in alignment with His Word. In other words, resist the temptation to pray fearful prayers. If fear has touched your heart as it did the hearts of Jehoshaphat and the people of Judah, pray the way they did—in faith believing that God would bring deliverance: "O Lord, God of our fathers, are you not the God who is in heaven? ... Power and might are in your hand, and no one can withstand you. ... We have no power to face this vast army that is attacking us. We do not know what to do, but our eyes are upon you" (2 Chronicles 20:6,12). Also, when you pray, remember that it is a conversation, not a monologue. Be sure to quiet yourself enough to hear God speak when you pray.

• **Stand in faith.** Both James and the apostle Paul admonish us to "stand firm in our faith." God told the people of Judah the same thing, "Stand firm and see the deliverance the Lord will give you" (2 Chronicles 20:17) If you are faced with a trying situation, God has deliverance in mind for you. He has promised not to leave us hopeless or abandoned. Standing firm in the light of God's truth is the right step toward victory, peace, and joy. The people of Judah marched out to battle singing because they knew their faith resided in an eternal God who had promised never to fail them.

• **Listen for prophetic guidance.** The Word says that, "Surely the Sovereign Lord does nothing without revealing his plan to his servants the prophets" (Amos 3:7), for "God does speak—now one way, now another—though man may not perceive it" (Job 33:14). Along with the Word, one of the ways God speaks is through godly men and women with prophetic insight and gifting. If they are responsible with their gifting, they can offer us great insight into what God is saying about and intending for our given situation. The Holy Spirit will also guide and direct us prophetically in the way that the Lord has called us to go. As we listen for prophetic guidance, we need to make sure that the message we hear always lines up with God's Word. A true prophetic word will never be in opposition to the truth of God. Here are some questions to ask about prophetic guidance:

1) It is biblical?
2) Is it confirmed by a number of people?
3) Is it consistent with what I feel the Holy Spirit is saying to me?
4) Do I have an inner peace about it?

• **Worship, worship, worship.** No matter what your situation may be ... be a Worshiper of God. Remember that He is totally aware of every aspect of your life. He knows when the sun is shining because He has set it in its place. Likewise, he knows when your life and heart are growing dim. In Candles in the Dark, Amy Carmichael writes, "We are never staying in the valley or the rough water; we are always only passing through them, just as the bride in the Song of Songs is seen coming up from the wilderness leaning upon her Beloved. So whatever the valley is, or however rough the waters are, we won't fear. Leaning upon our Beloved we shall come up from the wilderness and, as Psalm 84:6 says, 'Passing through the Valley of Weeping, they make it a place of springs.' We have found the living waters there and drink deeply [in God's presence.]" Worship the Lord at every turn in life, "Worship the Lord and listen to his voice, and if you do not rebel against the Lord's commands, and ... follow the Lord your God, then all will be well" (1 Samuel 12:14).

• **Collect the plunder.** Once Judah's enemies had destroyed one another, God's people were free to go onto the battlefield and retrieve all the "plunder" that had been left by the enemy. When they went to carry it away they found "a great amount of equipment and clothing and also articles of value—more than they could take away. There was so much plunder that it took three days to collect" (2 Chronicles 20:25). This would be like God saying to us, "You were obedient and lived by faith today and you really worshiped at the service on Sunday, so I'm going to open up the mall and all the surrounding stores for you and everyone at your church for three days. Just take anything you want free of charge." I'd be running to Best Buy and Guitar Center for gear, Home Depot for stuff for my house, and I'd make multiple trips to Gap, Banana Republic and Old Navy to fill up my SUV with clothes. Then I'd look to see if the offer was available on-line and bid $0.00 for item after item on eBay. I would be thanking God the whole time for the blessing. But I also know the struggle that would ensue from the distraction of having so much stuff. The apostle Paul writes that we should be "those who use the things of the world, as if not engrossed in them" (1 Corinthians 7:31). I know that even with the little bit of stuff I have, it's hard for me to keep from getting caught up in buying, playing with and maintaining it all. Sometimes I feel like a kid whose parents buy him wonderful Christmas presents to show their love and he gets so engrossed with the presents that he neglects his parents. The very thing that was meant to be an expression of love can end up actually suppressing the loving relationship. That makes me appreciate even more how Jehoshaphat and the people of Judah responded to the incredible gifts of victory, deliverance, and huge material blessing. The day after they collected all the plunder, "They gathered in the Valley of Blessing, which got its name that day because the people praised and thanked the Lord there. Then they returned to Jerusalem, with Jehoshaphat leading them, full of joy that the Lord had given them victory over their enemies. They marched into Jerusalem to the music of harps, lyres, and trumpets and pro-

> The very thing that was meant to be an expression of love can end up actually suppressing a loving relationship.

ceeded to the Temple of the Lord" (2 Chronicles 26-28). They weren't focusing on their enemy's demise or the things they accumulated. Judah carried the spoils of battle back to Jerusalem, but they did not forget to thank God for His blessing and mercy. In fact, they went straight back to their "church" and had another worship service. They continued to turn to God, the first thing they had done and now the last as well.

Many times, especially after we have been through a rough time, God sends blessings as a way of encouraging us and reminding us of His love. These are the times when we can take a deep breath and enjoy God's goodness, but we also have to guard our hearts so that we do not become either proud of or distracted by what we have. We need to remember that God is the giver of all good things. He is the source of our blessing and the object or our praise.

## "ATTACK" MUSICIANS

God is intent on getting the message out about the power of "war-ship." I was watching the news one night and with a "slip of the tongue" a CNN commentator announced to the world God's strategy for war. Reporting from Washington, D.C. on September 21, 2001, the reporter said that along with B-52 bombers, "We are sending F-16 fighter planes, which travel at supersonic speeds and carry air to air and air to ground attack musicians." She quickly corrected her statement to say "munitions."

However, the message couldn't be clearer. The same weapon that defeated the enemies of Judah is available to us today. When we sing and play God's praises, it goes into the air to move heaven and out into the earth to move people to win the battle for God's purposes.

## NO FEAR

Looking at the victory of Jehoshaphat and the "No Fear" worship team over a fear-o-cious enemy can help us overcome fear. Fear is the enemy's number one tool against the believer. He uses it to immobilize us and to bully us into giving up and throwing in the towel. However, I've noticed that he always overplays his hand. Satan knows that he is ultimately defeated, so he keeps pushing and pushing, desperately trying to grab some ground. If we hold fast to God in the heat of the battle, God will help us see the escalating ploys of the enemy. When they are exposed for the lies and toothless threats that they are, we can face the enemy's powerless roar with the resounding truth of God's Word and the freeing resonance of the spirit of worship.

When my own life began to tumble out of control, one of my first thoughts was, "Oh, no. What am I going to do? How am I going to handle all of this pressure at this point in my life?" These are fear questions. Fear entices us to think in this direction. But Jehoshaphat's questions were Spirit directed: "What do you want us to do about this, God? Lord, how are you going to handle this?" And his declarations were truth and faith directed: "O Lord, God of our fathers, are you not the God who is in heaven? You rule over all the kingdoms of the nations. Power and might are in your hand, and no one can withstand you ... if calamity comes upon us, whether the sword of judgment, or plague or famine, we will stand in your presence ... and will cry out to you in our distress, and you will hear us and save us" (2 Chronicles 20:6, 9).

Before His death, Jesus told His disciples, "Peace I leave with you; my peace I give you. I do not give to you as the world gives. Do not let your hearts be troubled and do not be afraid" (John 14:27). He knew that once He was gone, fear would strike at the hearts of those He loved. That is why He told them that "the

Comforter (Counselor, Helper, Intercessor, Advocate, Strengthener, Standby), the Holy Spirit, Whom the Father will send in My name [in My place, to represent Me and act on My behalf], He will teach you all things. And He will cause you to recall (will remind you of, bring to your remembrance) everything I have told you" (John 14:24, AMP). When we worship in spirit and in truth we are aligning with the Holy Spirit to magnify the Lord, apply His Word, amplify His truth and defy Satan's lies. This drowns out the lies that the enemy tries to fill our minds with and fills us with "powerful God-tools for smashing warped philosophies, tearing down barriers erected against the truth of God, fitting every loose thought and emotion and impulse into the structure of life shaped by Christ" (2 Corinthians 10:5, The Message). When the father of lies berates, the Father of lights illuminates and obliterates his schemes through every good and perfect gift of the Holy Spirit and the word of truth. (James 1:16-18)

> When we worship in spirit and in truth we are aligning with the Holy Spirit to magnify the Lord, apply His Word, amplify His truth and defy Satan's lies.

Worshiping in alignment with God's spirit and the truth of His Word magnifies our faith. When fear reached out to touch the hearts of the people of Judah, they turned to God—and He told them twice to "have faith." God knew that they would need faith to stand against their enemies. Over 400 years later, the apostle Peter told God's people who were under attack to, "Give all your worries and cares to God, for he cares about what happens to you. Be careful! Watch out for attacks from the Devil, your great enemy. He prowls around like a roaring lion, looking for some victim to devour. Take a firm stand against him, and be strong in your faith" (1 Peter 5:6-9).

When the armies from Ammon, Moab, and Mount Seir were

roaring down their necks, God told the people of Judah to "stand firm and see the deliverance the Lord will give you, O Judah and Jerusalem. Do not be afraid; do not be discouraged. Go out to face them tomorrow, and the Lord will be with you" (2 Chronicles 17:20). When circumstances at work and in our personal lives threaten to devour us, God says, "stand firm in the faith; be [people] of courage" (1 Corinthians 16:13). In both these instances Scripture echoes the words of Moses to the Israelites as they faced tremendous fear in what seemed like certain annihilation. Standing between a rock and a hard place with the Red Sea on one side and the Egyptians on the other, He said, "Do not be afraid. Stand firm and you will see the deliverance the Lord will bring you today" (Exodus 14:14).

Two years ago, I began to pray for courage, and I quickly discovered that you only need courage if you have fears to overcome. If there is nothing in our life to be afraid of, there is no need for courage. Courage isn't the absence of fear; it is the ability to overcome fear. If we're really honest, we would all admit that we have fears. In order to be courageous people, we have to be willing to face and learn to overcome our greatest fears. Since God has started answering my prayers for courage, I have learned that fear:

- is to the demonic as faith is to the divine
- empowers the enemy
- keeps us from stepping out to receive the promises of God
- prevents us from becoming all that God has planned for us to be
- keeps us from enjoying God's blessings

The familiar acronym tells us that fear is just False Evidence Appearing Real.

On the other hand, faith—

- empowers God's work in our lives
- prepares us to receive and enjoy His blessings
- strengthens our hearts and encourages us to keep going

even when the going seems especially tough
- positions us to be used by God for His purpose and glory
- teaches us how to trust God even when life appears to fall apart

God is in control of every circumstance that touches our lives. He never slumbers or sleeps, and He is never out of control. (Psalm 121:3)

Fear tempts us to become self-focused and absorbed. It is very difficult to think of others when your thoughts are wrestling with fear. It's interesting that one of the tribes attacking the people of Judah in our story was the Meunites (or as I like to emphasize, the Me-unites). This obsession with "me" can attack our worship and churches and even affect the way we interpret the Bible. Since we have lost the singular (thee and thou) of the King James Version and have only "you" left to signify both singular and plural, we have a tendency to translate most of the "you" instances as singular. In the New Testament, "you" signifies plural almost three times the amount that it means the singular. Yet our worship, our church experience, and our life often tends to be much more about "me" than about "us." With our tendency toward individualism, is it any wonder that we struggle to become unified in corporate worship and community? The worship choruses of our culture have been "I Did It My Way," "To Love Yourself is the Greatest Love of All", and country music singer Toby Keith's tongue-in-cheek declaration, "I Wanna Talk about Me":

> I wanna talk about me
> Wanna talk about I
> Wanna talk about number one
> Oh my me my
> What I think, what I like, what I know,
> what I want, what I see

I like talking about you, usually , but occasionally
I wanna talk about me

Corporate worship can keep us from setting our hearts on ourselves and our issues. It moves us toward setting our hearts on God and trusting Him and His faithfulness. This devotional from the Daily Word, speaks about the rock-solid faithfulness of God:

Whatever the condition, whatever the need, whatever the demand, God supplies. This is my faith; this is my assurance from the indwelling Christ. If there is a need for money to meet some pressing obligation, God supplies. If there is a need for strength to be able to accomplish all that is before me, God supplies. If there is a need for divine order in mind, body, or affairs, God supplies. At all times, in all ways, by all means, God supplies.

I release all anxious, doubtful thoughts from my mind. God supplies—this is my faith. I know without a doubt that God is on my side, and will see me through every challenge. With God's help, I will always emerge victorious.

If a dear one needs to know this truth, I will stand firm in my faith, knowing the truth about him. God supplies all that is needful for all His children.

## HANDLING FEAR

In Philippians, Paul writes, "My God will meet all your needs according to his glorious riches in Christ Jesus" (4:19). Trust Him and you will be amazed at the blessings He will bring your way. A. B. Simpson challenges us to "dare to trust Him and we will find that He is true to His word." Worshiping in the toughest circumstances declares, "In God I trust."

God's Word is packed with scriptures that address the subject of fear and how to deal with it. I want to challenge you to pick up a good concordance and spend time with the Lord asking Him to show you the ones that you can apply to your own life. What you will find as you go through His Word is that you are not alone in your battle with fear and discouragement. All of God's saints had to face this subject at one point in their lives.

Before Joshua and the Israelites crossed over the Jordan River and positioned themselves to conquer the city of Jericho, God instructed Joshua by saying, "As I was with Moses, so I will be with you; I will never leave you nor forsake you. Be strong and courageous" (Joshua 1:5). The Lord repeated this command four times within the first chapter of the book of Joshua. In verse 9, He told him, "Be strong and courageous. Do not be terrified; do not be discouraged for the Lord your God will be with you wherever you go."

As the people marched around the wall of Jericho, it was the sound of trumpets blowing that sounded the depth of their faith. Each time they completed a turn around the wall, God commanded them to blow their trumpets. There was no talking, no arrows flying—just walking and praying and worshiping Him for what He was going to do. On the seventh day, the trumpets sounded, the people shouted and the wall collapsed. (Joshua 6:20) Just as God granted Israel the victory, He will do the same in your life, if you are willing to wait for His deliverance, be obedient to His command, and worship Him even in the difficult times of life. (Also read Joshua 8:1; 10:8; 10:25; 11:6)

When Jesus walked on the water, the disciples were afraid at the site of Him coming to them. Added to this scenario was the fact that a horrific storm had over taken their boat. They were frightened and sure that they would be swept away by the Sea of Galilee's waves. But Jesus came to them walking on the water and "immediately said to them: 'Take courage! It is I. Don't be afraid.'" These are His words to us today, especially when the storm clouds gather and we begin to be tossed about by the waves of our circumstances.

As the people of Judah marched into battle, they sang songs of faith and their hearts remained strong. Worship and praise to God keeps the eyes of our hearts set on the One who alone has the ability to save us from the enemy's attacks. The same hope fulfilled in Judah is ours today.

American president Franklin D. Roosevelt wasn't speaking merely worldly wisdom when he said, "The only thing we have to fear is fear itself—nameless, unreasoning, unjustified terror which paralyzes needed efforts to convert retreat into advance" (First Inaugural Address, March 4, 1933). When we're immobilized by discouragement and fear, worship can mobilize us and convert our retreat into advance.

*Lord Jesus, I know that there have been times when my mind has been caught up with only one thing and that is "What about me!" Please teach me how to look to You in trust and praise through every challenge of life. Instead of singing, I wanna talk about me, I want to learn how to sing along with King David, "Praise the Lord, O my soul; all my inmost being, praise his holy name. Praise the Lord, O my soul, and forget not all his benefits!" (Psalm 103:1-2).*

## Chapter Seven

# The Un-Chained Gang

experiencing freedom & salvation through worship

*Sing to the Lord a new song,*
*For he has done marvelous things;*
*His right hand and his holy arm*
*Have worked salvation for him.*

PSALMS 98:1

For a number of years, we've had twice a month evenings of worship and prayer. We come before God with no agenda, just open hearts to worship Him. As we worship, we wait on God and pray as His Spirit stirs us.

On one of these evenings, I sensed that God wanted to minister CPR to us. For days, the Spirit had brought the initials CPR to my mind. Each time, I sensed these stood for Contentment, Praise, and Redemption. Before I had an opportunity to share what I had been feeling, one of the men at the meeting came up to our "open mic" and said something like "the Lord wants us to be content in Him and to praise Him in every circumstance." At this point that I stood up and confirmed his message, explaining how the Spirit had given me the CPR illustration of the very same message.

It became clear to me that God is challenging us to contentment and praise, which leads to redemption.

• **Contentment.** God wants us to be content and trust Him regardless of our circumstance. He wants us to learn how to rest in Him and look to Him for our every need instead of searching for satisfaction from other sources. When we approach life and what it hands us with contentment, we no longer relate to God on the basis of want, but on the basis of thanksgiving which is the key to the gates of His presence. Contentment with thanksgiving leads us to praise.

• **Praise.** When our faith is anchored in Christ, then our circumstances are under His control. No matter what winds of adversity blow hard against us, if we can enter His courts "with praise," then we can experience standing in His wondrous presence (Psalm 100:4) and receive the release of His power in our lives, which leads to redemption.

• **Redemption.** One Sunday during a worship service, God showed me a picture of our people stopping at booths outside our auditorium. These booths were similar to the ones in the airport where travelers can exchange their money for foreign currency before visiting a different country. When we praise God, we are exchanging the currency of this fallen world—our weaknesses, our sin, our troubles and our self-sufficiency—for the eternal currency of Heaven. The booths at the airport exchange our money for equivalent amounts in foreign currencies and tack on a carrying charge but with God's great exchange, He gives us infinite value and has paid all the fees with the sacrifice of His Son on the cross. In response, we can demonstrate our belief in the redemptive gift of Christ through our worship and praise. We can sing a song of trust in the One who has said that His grace is sufficient for every need we have (2 Corinthians 12:9) no matter what we may be going through.

Once we grasp this concept, we will become lighthouses to

those who are lost in the midst of the storm. We will lift up Jesus, the light of the world, and see all men and women drawn to Him. This is the glory of His redemption in our lives, circumstances, and in the hearts of those around us. It is the unconquerable strength that allows us to proclaim with the apostle Paul: "For to me, living is Christ and dying is gain." (Philippians 1:21, NRSV). This says that we trust God for everything, knowing that our temporal life is in His hands and our eternal life is the ultimate reward.

Steve Camp puts it this way, "It is easy to praise the Lord from the heights of His love, but it is richer to worship Him from the depths of His love. If you are in a time of testing or trial may I encourage you to stop and worship the Lord and to find comfort in His Word. The obedience that comes from surrendering your will and rights to Him brings peace and contentment. Job prayed in the course of his trials, 'Though He slay me, I will hope in him' (Job 13:15)." Our Lord is sovereign. He is in control of all things and there is mercy, grace, and eternal hope for all who come to worship Him.

## INTENT ON CONTENTMENT

The Apostle Paul had lost all of his freedom. He sat in the confinement of house arrest and still penned these amazing words, "I have learned to be content whatever the circumstances. I know what it is to be in need, and I know what it is to have plenty. I have learned the secret of being content in any and every situation, whether well fed or hungry, whether living in plenty or in want. I can do all things through [Christ] who gives me strength" (Philippians 4:11-13). Notice that he focuses on what he does have and not on what he doesn't have. The secret to Paul's contentment is found in 4:4-7: "Rejoice in the Lord always. I will say it again: Rejoice! ... The Lord is near. Do not be anxious about anything, but in everything, by prayer and petition, with thanksgiving, present your requests to God. And the peace of God, which transcends all understanding, will guard your hearts and your minds in Christ Jesus."

Later in Romans, he wrote, "We know that in all things God works for the good of those who love him, who have been called according to his purpose" (8:28). Many Christians sincerely believe that if their faith is strong enough, God will "keep" them from heartache and suffering. This certainly was not the case in Paul's life, and he was one of God's choicest servants. Few of us can relate to the depth of the suffering that he experienced. But he had a perspective that saw with the eyes of Heaven. He was able to walk in his circumstance, but still say, "Yet what we suffer now is nothing compared to the glory he will give us later" (Romans 18:18, NLT).

These weren't just lofty sounding words for Paul, he actually lived them out. An astounding example of this is the story that I mentioned earlier about his imprisonment along with Silas—his partner in ministry (Acts 16). When they cast a fortune-telling demon out of a slave girl and ruined her ability to make money for her owners, a riot ensued. "The crowd joined in the attack against Paul and Silas, and the magistrates ordered them to be stripped and beaten. After they had been severely flogged, they were thrown into prison, and the jailer was commanded to guard them carefully. Upon receiving such orders, he put them in the inner cell and fastened their feet in the stocks" (Acts 16:22-24). I would expect to be admired, blessed, and prospered from ministry as powerful and fruitful as that of Paul and Silas. Instead, they found themselves imprisoned, locked in stocks and stuck in a dark inner cell. Their backs were ripped from the severe beatings they had endured. From a human standpoint, there was no hope of deliverance.

It would be understandable for them to be groaning and

complaining about their condition, but, "about midnight Paul and Silas were praying and singing hymns to God, and other prisoners were listening to them." Instead of succumbing to the present possibility that "this was it" and that they would surely die, they began to praise God with enough boldness that their captive audience of fellow prisoners could hear. There were no signs of pity parties or lamenting about their circumstances even though the conditions were the worst.

Recently, I helped with some ministry on a cruise ship. Having spent four days in luxury and opulence, nearly everyone was complaining that the temperature when we arrived back in port was a "life-threatening" 48 degrees Fahrenheit. As a car pulled along the curb to pick up an elderly woman next to me, I decided to carry her luggage and load it into the car. In response the woman said, "You are the nicest man I have ever met." She then reached up, grabbed my face and kissed my cheek. I received it not as affection and praise for me, but as the heart response that people have when we worship God with our lives as well as our words, our actions as well as our declarations, and our service as well as our singing. As meager as any of our worship offerings may seem to us, it will inspire people to "kiss the Son" and offer praise to the real kindest man ever, Jesus.

In the midst of far greater hardship than the cool winter breeze that I endured, Paul and Silas didn't whine with voices of complaint, grumbling, or fear; they sang loudly to the glory of God. And God heard their songs.

The worship songs Paul and Silas were singing could have easily been the Hallels. These are the psalms of praise that the community of Israel recited at the great feasts or in the morning. They are Psalms 113 to 118, 136, and 146 to 150. Like the songs of the slaves we talked of earlier, they point the way to deliverance from oppression. When we look at the words to these hallelujahs, it's not hard to imagine the passionate singing of Paul and Silas:

I love the Lord, for he heard my voice; he heard my cry for mercy. Because he turned his ear to me, I will call on him as long as I live. The cords of death entangled me, the anguish of the grave came upon me; I was overcome by trouble and sorrow. Then I called on the name of the Lord: "O Lord, save me!" ... when I was in great need, he saved me.

— Psalm 116:1-6

I can imagine them getting to Psalm 114:7:

Tremble, O earth, at the presence of the Lord, at the presence of the God of Jacob ...

The biblical account tells us that the presence of God was so strong that it rocked the earth to the point where "suddenly there was such a violent earthquake that the foundations of the prison were shaken. At once all the prison doors flew open, and everybody's chains came loose" (Acts 16:26). When we sing God's praises and declare His word, it aligns us with Him and amplifies His power. Paul and Silas were so aligned with the presence of God through praise that it literally shook their world.

When we align with God through praise, it moves Him, it moves heaven, it moves earth, and it shines His light in the darkest of places. Worship leader and songwriter John G. Elliotte writes, "Worship music is powerful because it reminds Satan and his demons what they gave up." This is a disorienting torment to the kingdom of darkness. When Paul and Silas praised in their prison, it so aligned with and illuminated God's Word and His kingdom that not only were Paul and Silas set free, but it also brought salvation to those who were listening to them as they worshiped. When we worship God, it brings God's glory to us and brings victory, freedom, and salvation to others.

Why were Paul and Silas able to worship God in the worst of circumstances?

- **They knew God**—who He is and what He can do.
- **They knew the presence of God**—regardless of their circumstances, they were in His hands.
- **They knew the Word of God**—and they believed it. They decided that the suffering that they were called to endure offered the perfect opportunity for them to sing God's Word back to Him. They remained steadfast in the knowledge from the Word that God is loving and He is strong. (Psalm 62:11-12)

Jack Hayford writes: "The relationship between their song of praise and their supernatural deliverance through the earthquake cannot be overlooked. Praise directed toward God can shake open prison doors! A man was converted, his household saved, and satanic captivity overthrown in Philippi. Today, as well, praise will cause every chain of bondage to drop away. When you are serving God and things do not go the way you planned, learn from this text. Praise triumphs gloriously!"

When the situation of Paul and Silas was at its worst, their knowledge of and commitment to the Word of God guided them past their present physical suffering. As Jewish men from 2,000 years ago, they would have memorized Psalm 95:

> Come, let us sing for joy to the Lord;
> let us shout aloud to the Rock of our salvation.
> Let us come before him with thanksgiving
> and extol him with music and song.
> For the Lord is the great God,
> The great King above all gods.
> Come, let us bow down in worship,
> let us kneel before the Lord our Maker;
> for he is our God and we are the people of his pasture,
> the flock under his care.
>
> — Psalm 95:1-3, 6-7

The truth in these verses was not merely on the surface of these men's lives so that it could be washed away by the waves of torture and torment inflicted on them. These truths of God were embedded deep in their souls. When the blows of the whip tore away their flesh, their knowledge of God was not ripped away. They knew and trusted their God and His Word. Even in the deepest, darkest hour of his life and ministry, Paul worshiped according to the Word.

Psalm 95 describes worship by telling us:

- **What to do in worship**— "Come, let us sing for joy to the Lord" (v. 1a).
- **How to do it**—"Let us shout aloud to the Rock of our salvation" (v. 1b). (Worship is an active process.)
- **The attitude we should have as we worship**—"Let us come before him with thanksgiving" (v. 2a).
- **Who we worship**—Christ, our Lord and Savior. "Extol him with music and song" (v. 2b).
- **Why we worship**—"For the Lord is the great God, the great King above all gods" (v.3). "For he is our God and we are the people of his pasture, the flock under his care" (v. 7).

Paul echoed the words from this Psalm in his letter to the church at Colosse, reminding them from his knowledge of the Word, what worship is all about:

Let the word of Christ dwell in you richly (our *foundation* of worship) as you sing psalms, hymns, and spiritual song (our *activity* of worship) with gratitude in your hearts to God (our *attitude* of worship) and whatever you do, whether in word or deed, do it all in the name of the Lord Jesus (our *lifestyle* of worship) giving thanks to God the Father (the *object* of our worship) through him (our *access* to worship).

— Colossians 3:16-17
(parentheses mine)

## IS THAT YOU, GOD?

Once while my family was visiting the Grand Canyon, our young son, Robbie, was standing on the edge of a three-foot-high wall. He faced the edge and took on this "I'm Superman" posture and started to jump off. As I yelled to him "Robbie, don't jummm...", he did. On the way off, his foot caught the edge sending him head first onto a small but sharp rock. We rushed him to the Grand Canyon clinic. While waiting for treatment, he looked up with tears in his eyes and a big gash in his forehead and said to us, "I thought God would protect me." With the wisdom God gives to mothers in times of great need, my wife said, "He did try to protect you by giving you parents who told you not to jump." While we acknowledged that God did keep him from getting hurt worse, we have often unashamedly pointed to the scar on his forehead reminding our son that protection resides in knowing and following God's ways, especially obeying parents.

Many times, we are tempted to wonder the same thing Robbie did. We end up in painful circumstances and may think that God did not keep us safe. Often we don't recognize or acknowledge how God has protected us. Jude tells us that God "is able to keep you from falling and to present you before his glorious presence without fault and with great joy" (vs. 24). The meaning of "keep you from falling" here has to do with our salvation in Christ, but we also can surmise that the God who created us, knows all about us, has a future planned for us, and loves us can "keep" us in the midst of trouble. We may encounter hurt and sorrow along the way, but He has promised to preserve us for His glory.

In her book *The Hiding Place*, Corrie Ten Boom recounts the years she spent in one of Hitler's concentration camps. In the midst of the most horrific circumstances, she and her sister, Betsie, secretly held nightly prayer meetings. Betsy would urge

Corrie to join her in thanking God in all things. They would even pray for their captors, but Corrie insisted that she could not thank God for the misery inducing fleas that infested their barracks. She finally gave in and thanked God, only to realize later that the guards rarely ventured inside for fear of being bitten by the fleas. This was their only respite, offering them freedoms they would not have had otherwise. As Corrie struggled and her faith seemed to ebb, Betsie reminded her of a truth that became a cornerstone to Corrie's faith, "There is no pit so deep that God's love is not deeper still."

These words changed Corrie's life and attitude. She began to pray, worship, and teach God's Word with a sense of freshness and hope. Many of the women in her barracks accepted Christ as their Savior as a result of Corrie and Betsie's witness. Betsie died in Ravensbruck, but Corrie lived and was eventually released due to a "mistake" in paper work. Corrie wrote:

Following Betsie's death, God's presence was even more real. Even though I was looking into the valley of the shadow of death, I was not afraid. It is in times like these that Jesus comes the closest, taking our hand, and leading us through. One week before the order came to kill all the women of my age, I was free. I still do not understand all the details of my release from Ravensbruck. All I know is, it was a miracle of God.

Worship is never based on our circumstances. It is based on knowing the one true God who has promised never to leave us. It is based on us believing:

• **Who God is**—Faithful forever (Psalms 146:6), abounding in love. (Psalms 86:15)

• **How He works**—He is the Rock, His works are perfect, and all His ways are just. A faithful God who does no wrong.

(Deuteronomy 32:4)

• **That He works for the good in everything** (Romans 8:28)

> Worship God if you want the best; worship opens doors to all his goodness.
>
> — Psalm 34:9, The Message

During times of trouble or uncertainty, we often sing the song "You Are in Control," a musical version of Psalm 23. By worshiping and singing this song, we confirm the Word of God, affirm His presence, and hold firm to the character of God (who He is and what He does). Wherever you are in your life right now, reflect on the attributes and actions of God from these lyrics:

> You are my shepherd, [holding firm to who God is]
> I have no needs [He provides everything for us]
> You lead me by peaceful streams
> And You refresh my life [affirming God's ability and presence in your life]
> You hold my hand [holding firm and believing that God is our refuge and strength, an ever-present help in trouble — Psalm 46:1-3]
> and You guide my steps [confirm the Word — Your Word is a lamp to my feet – Psalm 119:105]
> I could walk through the valley of death
> And I won't be afraid
> Because You are in control [hold firm to the sovereignty of God. "Our God is a God who saves; from the sovereign Lord comes escape from death" (Psalm 68:20)]

Since God's Word is our source of truth, if we are to worship in spirit and in truth, our worship must be directed by and aligned with His Word. Worshiping without being founded on the word is like driving a car without a steering wheel. You may get going pretty fast, but it won't guide you where you need to go or allow you to steer past any obstructions in the road ahead.

Paul encourages the believers in Thessalonica to "be joyful always; pray continually; give thanks in all circumstances, for this is God's will for you in Christ Jesus" (1 Thessalonians 5:16). Freedom and salvation are the results of worshiping according to who the word says God is. Like it did for Paul and Silas, our obedience in worshiping in the middle of pain and discouragement will release God's power to set us free and to break the chains of those around us.

*Lord Jesus, I confess at times the pressures of life build up and I find that I either want to run or quit. Thank you for the testimony of the apostle Paul that has shown me how to endure and to turn to you for the hope I need. Help me to worship You with an open and obedient heart, knowing the truth that the Lord God is a sun and shield; the Lord bestows grace and favor and glory! No good thing does He withhold from those who walk uprightly ... blessed are those who trust in you - leaning and believing on You, committing all and confidently looking to You, and that without fear or misgiving! (from Psalms 84:11-12 AMP/NIV).*

# Chapter Eight

# A Community in Unity

unison and harmony in worship

*How good and pleasant it is
when God's people live together in unity!*

PSALMS 133:1

Once, when New York Philharmonic conductor Leonard Bernstein was asked what is the instrument in the orchestra most difficult to play, he answered, "Second fiddle." We've talked quite a bit already of Paul's significant influence, but much of it was supported and greatly enhanced by the participation of Silas. Silas is also probably the Silvanus who traveled with Peter and helped him write the letter we know as first Peter. He is a stellar example of creating the beautiful harmony of "second fiddle."

In an orchestra, second violins sit back behind the first violins and round out the sound of the other more prominent instruments. They create the beauty of harmony and the fullness of unity the way those who serve without being seen do and, unacknowledged, create harmony and beauty in the body of Christ. Our ability to contribute to the kind of unity that brings God's blessing is related to our graciousness and humility both when we are praised and when we don't get the praise we would like.

Recently, I was invited to speak about worship with a group of pastors. I asked them, "What are the most significant issues and needs that you have concerning your worship leaders?" Not one of them said that they wished their worship leaders would buy more equipment or come up with more creative styles of worship. None of them said they wished their leaders had learned to play their instruments better. Instead, these pastors said that if they had their deepest desire, it would be to see their worship leaders and teams grow in spirituality, discipleship, and relational wholeness. In other words, spiritual unity with God and harmony with others in their churches. Without hesitation, these pastors indicated that they knew healthy relationships were key to effective worship.

Along with the power of praise from a thankful heart, one of the greatest worship weapons we have is unity and harmony within the body of Christ. Psalm 133 says, "How good and pleasant it is when God's people live together in unity! It is like precious oil poured on the head, running down on the beard, running down on Aaron's beard, down upon the collar of his robes. It is as if the dew of Hermon were falling on Mount Zion. For there the Lord bestows his blessing, even life forevermore." This unity brings about three things:

- Anointing and commissioning for ministry (the oil)
- Refreshing (the dew)
- God's blessing

## THE OPPORTUNITY FOR UNITY IN COMMUNITY

*The Expositor's Bible Commentary* explains that "fellowship of God's people on earth is an expression of the priesthood of all believers, promised to Israel and renewed to the church in Christ (1 Peter 2:9-10) ... The specific reference to 'Aaron' should not be limited to him, as the whole priesthood was anointed with oil."

As believers, we are all priests and we can all receive the anointing, refreshing, and blessing that comes when we are in unity.

It is no coincidence that in music, the effectiveness of a worship song or hymn is completely dependent on how well the musicians play and sing in rhythmic and tonal unison and harmony. I repeatedly "beat the drum" over how important musical dynamics are to our worship teams. But, if any of us are marching to the beat of a different drum in our relational dynamics, we're just beating our heads against a wall.

Worship is an expression of our relationship with God. But, Christ also tells us, "If you are offering your gift at the altar and there remember that your brother has something against you, leave your gift there in front of the altar. First go and be reconciled to your brother; then come and offer your gift" (Matthew 5:23-24). Jesus says if our relationships aren't in unity and harmony—forget about worship until we get them straight. It doesn't matter how great our vocal harmonies sound, if were not in relational harmony, it's discordant.

Though it's essential to have unity with God and with those around us, it doesn't mean we are to all look, act, think, or dress alike or agree on everything. We are to have unity with diversity. God made us each with different personalities and gifts. We need to honor one another, defer to one another, respect one another and just basically love one another. In talking about our worship and relationship, Paul tells the church in Rome, "Be devoted to one another in brotherly love. Honor one another above yourselves" or as it says in the Message, "Be good friends who love deeply; practice playing second fiddle" (Romans 12:10). He knew that unity in the church is broken when we allow our opinions and ambitions to take precedence over love, let disagreements linger, or leave conflicts unresolved. Many physicians and psychologists believe that most of the illnesses we suffer from can be traced back to feelings of anger, fear, dread, and disappointment. Broken unity leads to broken hearts, broken fellowship, broken ministry, and broken churches. When this happens, something inside of us is altered. Our lives don't hum along in the right key. Then when we enter a time of worship, whether it is corporal or personal, it's going to be strident.

In our church and worship arts community, we have five important principles that have helped keep our worship flowing and our relationships in tune:

**Keep short accounts.** Don't let offenses or hurts build up. When conflicts happen, get them resolved right away.

**Act in the opposite spirit.** If you feel someone is being harsh with you, be extra kind to them. If they are angry, demonstrate peace and patience.

**Ask questions rather than making accusations.** Ask, "Are you troubled, having a difficult time, or struggling about something?" This creates a dialogue rather than a war.

**Avoid creating win/loose situations.** Don't take the "Who is right, who is wrong" approach. Share feelings and be willing to compromise on your desires as long as the result is still godly.

**Be willing to own your part of the conflict.** "It takes two to tango." Very rarely is a conflict totally the result of only one person's issues. Be a beam in-speck-tor. Be willing to look at the beam in your own eye (your issues and contribution to a conflict) before you point out the speck in someone else's eye (their issues and contribution to a conflict).

## "I JUST WANT TO BE SURE OF YOU"

*Piglet sidled up to Pooh from behind.*
*"Pooh!" he whispered.*
*"Yes, Piglet?"*
*"Nothing," said Piglet, taking Pooh's paw. "I just wanted to be sure of you."*

In our increasingly insecure and unstable world, we all just want to be sure that God and others are there for us. We no longer expect our governments or societies to provide the consistency and stability we need, so our hearts cry out to be accepted and unconditionally loved by God, our families, and our church family. With many of us facing some sort of crisis, significant life change or family issues, our worship and relationships within the church can provide a desperately needed bastion of comfort and support. Ever since 9/11, the tsunami and Hurricane Katrina, I have become increasingly aware of the need for greater unity and community in our church family. My wife had a song on the CCM charts a while back called "We Need Each Other" that she recorded with Marty McCall from the group "First Call" and a pre-"Butterfly Kisses" Bob Carlisle. Their voices blended together representing the harmony and unity needed in the body of Christ as they sang these words by Walt Harrah and Claire Cloninger:

> Sometimes I feel so alone
> So tired of fighting it on my own
> Tired of this race is there a place I can run to
> Open your heart and you'll see
> You are a part of a family
> This is the way we were intended to be
> Bound by faith in a Kingdom above
> Standing shoulder to shoulder in love
> I need you
> And you need me
> And together we'll face the world as God's forgiven family
> We are children of one father
> We are sisters we are brothers
> And we need each other

117

When we open ourselves up to and recognize our need for others in the body of Christ, we can live this kind of supportive life together. But, allow that unity to be broken and life suddenly turns unstable, vulnerable, and emotionally risky.

Trace and I traveled extensively in our music ministry with our two children in tow. We had a great time as a family, but as siblings are prone to do, our kids would sometimes get into squabbles. While cruising down the highway, I would call to the rear of our motor home, "Don't make me come back there." As a father, I wanted my children to get along. Our heavenly Father wants us, as His children, to get along as well. As we take our worship journey together, motoring along each week in our "church home," how can we keep our heavenly Father from having to say, "Don't make Me come down there"?

• **First, we must come before Him with an open heart.** We may be in the middle of worship and the Lord brings an issue to mind that happened years or months ago. Addressing an issue with an offended or offending person may not be immediately possible, but dealing with it in the presence of God is of utmost importance to breaking through the barriers to unity. We can say, "Lord, thank You for bringing this to my mind. I know that I've not dealt with this and need Your help in order to go forward. Please forgive me for clinging to the memory, the anger, or the frustration. Show me how to handle the situation and then give me the strength to follow through."

• **Second, there may be issues surrounding our lives that would make it impossible to go back to the person who hurt us.** Those who have suffered abuse should know that Jesus Christ is their ever present Savior and God. He understands what it means to be rejected, abused, forgotten, left out, and abandoned. Without a doubt, we can turn to Him and find the healing our hearts need for every hurt and betrayal. Then, we need to release any bitterness we have toward those who have hurt us.

It's been said that unforgiveness and bitterness are poisons we drink hoping to make someone else sick. Though people have most likely hurt us, we still need to practice forgiveness in order to be free: "When you stand praying [or worshiping], if you hold anything against anyone, forgive him, so that your Father in heaven may forgive you your sins" (Mark 11:25).

• **Third, if we are the ones who have offended another, we need to realize that our words may not be met with total understanding.** A light of unity may have been switched on in our own lives, but the people hearing what we have to say may need time to adjust to the sudden illumination.

• **Fourth, we have to want unity. Sadly, disunity can become a way of life for many of us who refuse to let go of the hurt we harbor.** Eventually it becomes a constant companion we enjoy entertaining, a miserable friend that becomes an excuse for not extending the love of Christ to those we meet and those we should have fellowship with. We may be afraid of getting hurt again, but when we are tempted to sacrifice unity for self-preservation or survival, let's let the love of Christ prevail and courageously choose to sing God's praises in harmony with those in our spiritual family.

## TUNING TO THE PERFECT PITCH

Picture a weekend service at your church. Just before it is time to start, everyone walks in carrying a large boombox turned up loudly. Now imagine the sound it would make if they were all tuned to a different station. The cacophony creates such dissonance that any attempt at worship or communication is swallowed up in the distracting noise. But if everyone was tuned to the same station that was broadcasting a worship song it would be greatly amplified. This is the dissonance of division or resonance of unity created when we come together to worship. Musically, dissonance is "a mingling of discordant sounds; especially, a clashing or unresolved musical interval or chord," but it is also "lack of agreement." Resonance is the "intensification and prolongation of sound, especially of a musical tone, produced by sympathetic vibration" but also a "richness . . . especially in evoking . . . strong emotion." When our hearts and lives resonate in harmony with God and unity with each other, our worship creates a rich atmosphere that stirs people's emotions and their spirits.

I remember once recording a track for a song and thinking that something sounded really weird. As I soloed each instrument, they each sounded fine. It took me a while to realize that one of my guitar parts was out of tune from the others. I had tuned the guitar to itself but not to the same reference pitch, so it created a dissonance with the other instruments. In our lives, the "reference pitch" is the Holy Spirit. He resonates with the mind of Christ and the Word of God. When we are all in tune with the Holy Spirit, our worship lifts up Jesus and magnifies God. An "out of tune" musical instrument always distracts the listener from whatever message the music is trying to convey. The same is true with us. When we are out of tune with the "reference pitch," the richness of our relationships will be diminished, distracting us and others in our worship of God.

> When we are all in tune with the Holy Spirit, our worship lifts up Jesus and magnifies God.

One morning as I was writing about the glorious, unhindered worship we have when our relationships are in harmony, I suddenly realized that I was thinking about a meeting that I had had with a colleague the previous day. I immediately became aware that I was offended and carrying some hurt. I also wondered if had offended him as well. I didn't immediately connect the unresolved conflict to my ability to worship freely, but it started to nag at me. After a couple of hours of procrastination, I was reminded again that it is much easier to write about resolving conflict than it is to do it. I knew in this case that I would need to express my personal hurt, apologize for my contribution to the misunderstanding, and be willing to risk rejection and being misunderstood. But I also knew that my life and ministry would not be as fruitful if I was a vessel contaminated by unresolved issues.

Whenever I hit a wrong note while leading worship, I can just shrug it off and go on. When I hit a wrong chord in a recording studio, I can easily erase it and re-record it. But when there is discordance in my relationships, it is not that easy. I realize that in this case my relationship, my worship, and even my success in writing this chapter would be hindered if I ignored what God was urging me to do—deal with disunity. I'll admit that I was relieved when I called and got his voice mail, but when we finally talked I apologized. Then he apologized. We cleared up the misunderstanding. The accusations of the enemy were undermined and I felt much freedom in worship. What a coincidence!

When a chord contains extra notes that are not in harmony with the others, it creates a sense of tension in the sound. Effective music or relationships isn't void of tension and discord. Tension and release are a normal part of music, just like conflict and resolution is a normal part of healthy relationships. Like with musical chords, unless the tension is released and resolved, there will be distraction and our ability to worship will be hindered.

Paul tells us, "If it is possible, as far as it depends on you, live at peace with everyone" (Romans 12:16). This means that we use all that we do, think, and say to resolve any conflict that is outstanding. John reminds us "we love because he first loved us. If anyone says, 'I love God,' yet hates his brother, he is a liar. For anyone who does not love this brother, whom he has seen, cannot love God, whom he has not seen. And he has given us this command: Whoever loves God must also love his brother" (1 John 4:19-21).

## QUICKSAND OR QUICK RESOLVE

In our marriage, Trace and I made a commitment to work together to resolve our conflicts as soon as possible. We take God's words seriously: "In your anger do not sin; and do not let the sun do down while you are still angry, and do not give the devil a foothold" (Ephesians 4:26-27). Years ago, we were having a "strong disagreement" and decided to finish our "conflict resolution" in the car before entering a store where we had planned to go shopping. After some discussion, we resolved the issue and headed into the store with our four-year-old son who had just endured our entire "discussion." A sales clerk approached us and our outgoing son blurted out, "This is my mom and dad. All they do is argue." Immaturity may see the process of conflict resolution as just plain arguing, but honesty and quick resolution to conflict is very important to maintaining godly, healthy relationships.

Whether you are married, on a worship team, or a member of a church, wherever there are human relationships, there will be conflicts. It is not whether you will have conflict or not. It is inevitable. The question is how you will handle them when they come.

*How do we get a relationship back on track once it is derailed?*

• **Lay the matter before the Lord.** He knows that unity is key to your worship and praise of Him. Ask Him to show you where you may have taken a wrong turn, said the wrong thing, or failed to be sensitive.

• **Be willing to resolve the conflict.** Often two of the most difficult words to say are "I'm sorry," but saying we are sorry for our part is often the key to starting the process to restore unity.

• **Be patient, be kind ... be loving.** Some conflicts are resolved immediately. There are other times when we have to be willing to wait. It may take the other person or persons a long time to accept and forgive, or they may never come around. God's command to be loving is not contingent on whether we are loved back.

• **Be aware of the enemy's schemes.** Our adversary, the devil, is always hurling accusations and lies in an attempt to divide and separate believers. The word "devil" means to throw or to thrust through. I have seen friends and marriages that should have lasted a lifetime dissolve all because Satan devised a plan to divide what God had brought together.

One of the ways to combat Satan's tactics is to speak the truth in love and respond to each other with humility. An opportunity for me to practice humility came through a refreshingly honest woman on the sound team at our church who spoke the truth in love. When she asked to speak with me, I thought that she was going to quit our sound team due to other obligations. Instead she said, "When you talk to me from the platform and order me around—saying things like 'turn this instrument down or up' or 'this mic isn't working,' I feel demeaned and disrespected." I had not really even considered the way I was speaking to her. Rehearsals and Sunday services can be very busy, so I thought I was just giving clear instruction and honoring the time the worship team spent waiting for the sound to be adjusted. However, I didn't realize I was being so uncaring with my words and instructions.

Rather than being sensitive to this woman as a person of value and worth, I was just getting the job done at her expense. Later, I told her that I didn't even realize what I was doing and that I appreciated her pointing this out to me. Once we dealt with the problem from a relational standpoint, the entire atmosphere changed. There was a new freedom in our rehearsals and in worship, and I am sure God was honored by our ability to work things out with Christ-like unity. Her willingness to resolve the conflict with loving confrontation greatly encouraged me to own my part. The enemy's plans to divide us were foiled and her gentle surgery to extract my insensitivity demonstrated that "faithful are the wounds of a friend" (Proverbs 27:6).

• **Be determined to go forward.** If the person who has offended you has done something immoral or been physically or extremely emotionally abusive, proceed with caution and wisdom, praying and seeking counsel from others about how to handle the situation. However, in most cases where physical or emotional abuse won't befall you, you should determine to move forward in the relationship, at least giving it one more try. Paul had a disagreement with Barnabas concerning John Mark. In Acts 15 we read, "They had such a sharp disagreement that they parted company. Barnabas took Mark and sailed for Cyprus, but Paul chose Silas and left ..." (v. 39-40). Paul believed that Mark had deserted the group earlier and did not want to run the risk of this happening again.

However, later we discover that the entire matter had been resolved because Paul writes to Timothy, "Do your best to come to me quickly ... Get Mark and bring him with you, because he is helpful to me in my ministry (2 Timothy 4:9, 11). Paul, Mark and probably Barnabas as well didn't let conflict keep them from unity in the faith or ministering together. We don't know the details of how, but somewhere along the journey Paul's relationship with Mark had been transformed and the enemy's ploy to separate these two godly men was totally defeated.

## HARD HAT AREA: UNITY UNDER CONSTRUCTION

A friend of mine, who is a well known pastor, came to speak at one of our church meetings. He is known as a man of character and integrity. If he gives you his word on an issue, you can count on him to fulfill it. However, as our meeting began, my friend didn't show up on time. The more we waited, the more concerned we became. Finally, we saw him coming through the doorway. Once he was up on the platform, he said, "I just want to tell you why I was late. My wife and I were having a conflict and I want to practice what I preach. Though I value greatly being on time for ministry, it would lack integrity for me to get up here and speak to you as a leader or as a man of God without resolving it with her. We worked through it, and we are OK now." I know it is not always possible to work through every conflict in our life completely before we minister, but the biblical principle is that God desires us to worship and serve with relationships intact and conflicts resolved.

Loving others is a prerequisite for true worship and ministry. The Word tells us that "if we don't love people we can see, how can we love God, whom we have not seen?" (1 John 4:20-21) and "If I could speak in any language in heaven or on earth but didn't love others, I would only be making meaningless noise like a loud gong or a clanging cymbal." (1 Corinthians 13:1, NLT).

What does worship enhancing love look like? We've all read it before, but let's look at the qualities of love from 1 Corinthians 13 as it relates to how we act and feel toward those we worship with, whether it's a fellow worship team member, someone in your small group, someone at church, or, like the woman who confronted me, a tender servant-hearted member of the sound team.

Love is patient, love is kind. It does not envy, it does not boast, it is not proud. It is not rude, it is not self-seeking, it is not easily angered, it keeps no record of wrongs. Love does not delight in evil but rejoices with the truth. It always protects, always trusts, always hopes, always perseveres. Love never fails.

— 1 Corinthians 13:2; 4-8

If we fail to love those around us, then one of the first things that suffer is our ability to freely worship the One who is love. Worship is love responding to love. "This is love: not that we loved God, but that he loved us" (1 John 4:10). We worship as a free flow of love for a God who loves us all. We interrupt the flow when we don't love those whom He loves. If blood flow is blocked to any part of our physical body, it soon ceases to function. Breaches in our relationships block the flow of God's presence and Spirit in our worship, and His full blessing is hindered in our lives.

That is why Paul exhorts us to, "Let there be real harmony so there won't be divisions in the church. I plead with you to be of one mind, united in thought and purpose" (1 Corinthians 1:10, NLT).

*Lord Jesus, thank You that you have called me your friend. (John 15:15-16, Proverbs 18:24) Teach me how I can be the kind of friend who loves at all times to my co-workers, fellow church members, neighbors and all those around me (Proverbs 17:17). Also, give me a willing and teachable heart so that I may learn how to build right relationships—the kind that join together in unity of spirit to honor and worship You.*

## Chapter Nine

# Up and Over

### overcoming relational hurdles to worship

*Therefore, if you are offering your gift at the altar*
*and there remember that your brother or sister*
*has something against you,*
*leave your gift there in front of the altar.*
*First go and be reconciled to that person;*
*then come and offer your gift.*

MATTHEW 5:23-24

*You told me that all of your angels and demons*
*Are constantly kicking and fighting and screaming*
*There's no light and there's no sound*
*Bet you wanna drag the sunrise down*
*You tell me it feels like you're running in circles*
*And all the time they keep raising the hurdles*
*Out of sight and under ground*
*You're dreaming you're gonna drag the sunrise down*
*Time is on your side*
*You hide behind the tainted smile*
*But it s there deep in your eyes*
*Drop the blade and look inside*
*Only you can find the light*

ROOSTER, "DRAG THE SUNRISE DOWN"

To keep our pathway to worship clear, it is imperative that we learn to overcome the obstacles and hurdles that can trip us up. Two great examples of overcoming obstacles are Moses and Nehemiah—Edwin Moses and Renaldo Nehemiah. For a decade in the 1970s and 1980s, Edwin Moses was the greatest 400-meter hurdler in the world, and Renaldo Nehemiah was a world-class 110-meter hurdler. Both men were strong runners, but people said that there were other runners who were stronger. Both were fast, but once again many said that there were other runners who were faster. So, why did these two men enjoy such success? They both had the ability to anticipate, approach, and overcome the obstacles placed in front of them. To be effective Olympians, they had to overcome the obstacles of hurdles. To be effective worshipers, we must overcome the obstacles of conflict.

## DON'T JUMP; CONFRONT

Whether we are an athlete or a Worshiper, there are three different approaches to the hurdles we face:

• **Avoidance.** When we avoid the conflict, it is as if we stop at a hurdle hoping that the obstacle will go away. But it doesn't. It just grows into walls in our lives, blocking the free flow of the spirit and distracting us from doing what God has called us to do—worship Him with an undivided heart and mind.

• **Attack.** When we go on the offensive or get defensive, we are trying to knock down the hurdles that are in our way. However, this only trips us up, and we quickly discover that this is not the way God wants us to deal with conflict either. Broken relationships are not healed by force. That only leads to being disqualified as it pronounces that "I am right and you are wrong," or "I am determined to defeat you with arguments."

• **Loving Confrontation.** The godly approach to conflict and disunity is "loving confrontation." This involves speaking the truth in love (Proverbs 27:6, NASB), listening for the guidance of the Holy Spirit, humbling ourselves before God and each other, and then asking Him to take control of the situation. It is basically where we take on the attitude of a servant—serving to bring about resolution through loving dialogue. When we come to this point, we are no longer interested in creating a "win" or "lose" situation. Instead, we are interested in godly unity. Having this type of attitude also helps us better understand Christ's words in Matthew 5:23-25 where He instructs us to settle disagreements with those around us.

Until we go to those whom we have offended or been offended by and settle any outstanding conflicts or issues, our worship will be hindered. Are there exceptions to this rule? Not really. However, God's timing is perfect. Don't panic after reading these words and rush out to tell 15 people that you know that you have done something to hurt them at some point and you want to ask for their forgiveness.

Instead, allow the Holy Spirit to guide you in your quest to be holy before God. Confess what you have done and ask Him to show you how to handle the situation and, most importantly, when. Usually, when God begins to move, He moves swiftly, but allow Him to lead. Also, be aware of falling prey to a sense of false guilt. Satan loves to belittle us and tempt us into believing that we have made a mistake that God cannot repair or restore. Nothing is beyond the Lord's grace, and nothing is too great for Him to handle. True guilt is a stepping-stone to godly conviction. You don't have to repeatedly seek God's forgiveness. Tell Him the heartache you have suffered at sin's hand. Pray for His forgiveness and then go forward to walk in the newness of His life in you. He will guide you to a point of restoration in your relationships and, more importantly, in your fellowship with Him. Then all of heaven will worship with you.

A foundational approach in how to handle getting over relational hurdles is to avoid accusations. The Bible calls Satan "the accuser of our brothers, who accuses them before our God day and night" (Revelation 12:10). When we make a point of accusing someone, we become aligned with the enemy's tactics. Instead, in order to settle some tough disagreements in a God-honoring way, we will have to draw each other out with questions and sharing of feelings instead of accusations. It also means that there will need to be some compromising on everyone's part. If sin, not just disagreement or conflicting goals, is involved, loving confrontation can help bring about conviction from the Holy Spirit, encourage repentance and avoid the condemnation of the enemy.

God wants us to learn how to confront one another in love, not attack or avoid. When I share how I feel about the conflict or problem and you share how you feel, relationship is born and together with the Lord, we can work through any problem we face. Part of healthy conflict resolution is avoiding using statements that assign motives like, "You are just selfish." Words like these can place the other person on the attack or the defensive and nothing is gained. Instead, we can say statements like, "When you say things like you just said, it makes me feel like my position or opinion is not valued."

> God wants us to learn how to confront one another in love, not attack or avoid.

Using "I feel" statements works because they are not about what is wrong with the other person or about how bad what they have done is. It allows them to respond and not argue, defend, or attack. It frees them to listen rather than forcing them to formulate a rebuttal. When I have approached others this way, the most frequent response I get is, "I'm sorry, it was not my intention to make you feel that way." This leads to open dialogue and restoration of relationship. Then you are free to add how you feel concerning the relationship with statements like, "If we allow this brokenness to continue, or this misunderstanding to go unresolved, we could become divided as friends." The enemy would love nothing more than to divide people and prevent believers from worshiping God together. But loving conflict resolution gets over the hurdles he places in our path.

In worship, both unison and harmony are effective. In unison, everyone sings the exact same notes. In harmony, we sing different notes that are complimentary to each other. This is true of life as well. There will be times when we are in complete unison with those around us and other times when we will harmonize. The goal always is to make beautiful music as we worship the Lord and glorify Him with our lives.

Where there is too much unison (melody only) without harmony, music becomes too simplistic and boring. It lacks color and depth. When there is too much complex harmony without unison, life or worship can become a cacophony of sound that strains the listener's ability to focus on the message.

In music, we want to have both unison and harmony. In the church, we want to have both unity and diversity. We need unity of spirit and purpose while maintaining a diversity of gifts, talents, and personalities. Unity doesn't demand that we all act alike or think the same way. Paul tells the church in Corinth that they "have the mind of Christ" (1 Corinthians 2:16). Later, he reminds them to "be of one mind, live in peace. And the God of love and peace will be with you" (2 Corinthians 13:11). This doesn't mean that we should all be identical; it means that we are all tuned to the same station, the Holy Spirit, who broadcasts the thoughts of heaven. This is the mind of Christ that compels us to love each other.

Isn't this what it is all about—loving others with the love of Christ and worshiping God in his blessing and grace? In

Philippians Paul writes, "If you have any encouragement from being united with Christ, if any comfort from his love, if any fellowship with the Spirit, if any tenderness and compassion, then make my joy complete by being like-minded, having the same love, being one in spirit and purpose. Do nothing out of selfish ambition or vain conceit, but in humility consider others better than yourselves" (1 Corinthians 2:1-3).

## SLICING UP THE HUMBLE PIE

Some of my friends had a band that they named "The Fabulous Humble Brothers." Like them, not taking yourself too seriously is one way to resist the tug of pride that is so pervasive in our culture, especially for those in music and the arts. If we struggle to take the high road to humility, friends can always help keep our pride in check, like the man who confessed to his friend, "You know I really struggle with pride," to which his friend replied, "What could you possibly have to be proud of?" But the truly best way to humility is to follow the example of Jesus. When it comes to humility, imitation of Jesus Christ is the sincerest form of worship. Paul admonishes us to "[t]hink of yourselves the way Christ Jesus thought of himself. He had equal status with God but didn't think so much of himself that he had to cling to the advantages of that status no matter what. Not at all. When the time came, he set aside the privileges of deity and took on the status of a slave and became human! Having become human, he stayed human. It was an incredibly humbling process. He didn't claim special privileges. Instead, he lived a selfless, obedient life and then died a selfless, obedient death—and the worst kind of death at that: a crucifixion" (Philippians 2:5-8, The Message).

To illustrate how important humility is to God, Jesus told this story:

Two men went up to the temple to pray, one a Pharisee and the other a tax collector. The Pharisee stood up and prayed about himself: "God, I thank you that I am not like other men—robbers, evildoers, adulterers—or even like this tax collector. I fast twice a week and give a tenth of all I get."

But the tax collector stood at a distance. He would not even look up to heaven, but beat his breast and said, "God, have mercy on me, a sinner." I tell you that this man, rather than the other, went home justified before God. For everyone who exalts himself will be humbled, and he who humbles himself will be exalted.

—Luke 18:10-14

True humility wins God's heart every time. The Pharisee was so sure of his self-righteous behavior that he approached God by announcing himself superior to the very people that Christ came to redeem. His prayers and any attempt to worship God were wasted on his desire to exalt himself. However, the tax collector was so aware of his sinful state that he could not even look up into the temple of God. He stood at a distance and prayed for God to have mercy on him.

I am on a leadership team of a group called UniteAtlanta, a movement of pastors, worship leaders, marketplace leaders, and intercessors. The Lord used me to help with the formation of this group, which has brought Christian leaders together from all denominations to pray, worship God, and reach the city. However, when it came to our largest event of the year, I was out of the country and could not be a part of it. In fact, I got off the airplane just in time to rush to the worship service.

As I entered the building, I realized that I was fighting feelings of feeling rejected, overlooked, left out, and that God had forgotten me. I struggled past these temptations and worshiped anonymously with the rest of the thousands of believers who had gathered in the arena. Though I was not on the platform, I chose to enjoy God's presence and rejoice that the body of Christ had come together that weekend to serve and worship Him. My heart was touched by God's Spirit, and I knew that not only was He doing a deep work with the church in our city, He was doing a deep work within me.

The next year we had the same conference, and I ended up being out of town until the day before the event. I had to show up and do the same thing, and I realized that God was testing me. He said to me, "Is this worship event only about you being on the platform or about you worshiping Me? Is it about you leading or can you join in worship as fully from row 127 as you could if you were in front leading worship?" I confess that once again I struggled with my feelings. But I knew that God had spoken to me, and regardless of where I was sitting, the goal of my heart became one of unity and worship. God is faithful to check and recheck our level of humility and sensitivity to His Spirit. He wants to expose whether or not we are truly willing to obey Him and worship Him with a humble heart, or if we have lingering feelings about "how great we are" that hinder us from proclaiming "How Great Thou Art"?

My testing continued. A few days later, I received a call from our youth pastor and he said, "Hey, we have a concert tomorrow night with four young bands, and the guy that usually runs sound can't do it. So, I was just wondering if you could help them set up." I was tempted to think, "I can't do this. I'm the worship leader; I'm an associate pastor; don't you know that?"

God spoke to me so clearly and reminded me that earthly titles reflect the things I get to do but that "who you are is a servant—go be one!" As I showed up the next evening, God opened a door for me to encourage the young bands that were there along will those who were running sound for them. I think that was more about worship leading than what I did on the platform the following Sunday.

When we humble ourselves before the Lord through prayer, praise, worship, and service, He blesses us abundantly with His mercy and grace. But it is our attitudes of honesty, humility, confession, and a contrite heart—not our actions – that make us acceptable before God. The Lord says, "I live in a high and holy place, but also with him who is contrite and lowly in spirit," and "I will bless those who have humble and contrite hearts" (Isaiah 57:15, NIV; 62:2, NLT). Contrite has the same meaning as a rock crushed so finely that its dust floats on water. When we are contrite in heart and spirit, we can be carried along in the river of God's presence. But when we resist Him and refuse to be crushed, we sink quickly to the bottom and the flow of His Spirit passes us by.

The classic story of the cracked pot sheds a redeeming light on our brokenness. It's about a water bearer in India who had two large pots, hung on each end of a pole which he carried across his neck. One of the pots had a crack in it, and at the end of the long walk from the stream to the master's house, the cracked pot would arrived only half full.

After two years of this, the poor cracked pot was ashamed that it wasn't like the other perfect pot. But the water bearer pointed out the beautiful flowers along the side of the path where the pot lost its water. He had planted flower seeds along the path knowing that the broken pots would water them. God plants seeds of opportunity to bring beauty out of our brokenness as we offer ourselves as broken vessels and pour ourselves out upon Jesus as an act of worship.

A world hungry for power and control views humility and brokenness as weakness. It's seen as the kind of character trait that could get you fired in the opening episode of "The Apprentice." But true humility is a form of godly strength. Being contrite and broken by God leads to Him using and directing us where He wants. It also releases God to fill these broken vessels that we are with the oil of His anointing and power. Until we humble ourselves before God, we cannot be broken, and until we are broken, we are of little use to the Lord. Peter reminds us that "God resists the proud but gives grace to the humble" (1 Peter 5:5).

Peter also goes on to provide words of hopeful insight: "Humble yourselves, therefore, under God's mighty hand, that he may lift you up in due time" (1 Peter 5:6). James writes, "Humble yourselves before the Lord, and he will lift you up" (James 4:10). When your circumstances have you so low that you feel as though you cannot even worship the Lord, as you bow down humble in heart and spirit, He will put His loving arms around you and lift you up. When you are tempted to feel like shouting "I am the king of the world" in pride or self-confidence, bow down and God will lift you up to your place in His kingdom—not to restore you to your "old" ways, but so you can serve Him and praise Him with a new song.

*Father, thank You for being patient with me—for loving me even when I do unlovely things. Thank You for caring enough to teach me how to live in unity with you and those around me. I dedicate my life to loving You and loving others as I worship and serve You with a humble and willing heart. Amen.*

# Chapter Ten

# A Passion for Purity
## seeing God for who He is in worship

*Give me one pure and holy passion*
*Give me one magnificent obsession*
*Give me one glorious ambition for my life*
*To know and follow hard after You*

MARK ALTROGEE, "ONE PURE AND HOLY PASSION"

I was surfing the web looking for a humorous story in preparation for a sermon and had hardly noticed that I had sifted through half a dozen off-color jokes and clicked past a few tantalizing pop-up ads. But then I felt strange coming back to write the sermon, especially since it was the same time that I was writing this chapter about purity. I felt a combination of slimed and convicted as I recognized my own sinfulness and that of our world in light of God's holiness and glory. Maybe it was just a small glimpse of what Isaiah experienced. He tells us about it as part of his description of a remarkable worship encounter he had when he saw God seated on the throne in His temple (Isaiah 6). He describes a multi-media experience with sights and sounds that overloaded his senses, but it was his response that brought such powerful meaning to being in the presence of God's glory. He heard angels saying, "Holy, holy, holy is the Lord Almighty; the whole earth is full of his glory." He saw the blinding light of God's glory and he felt the doorposts and thresholds shake. In the overwhelming presence of God, Isaiah was shaken and fell on his face in fear as he cried out, "Woe to me! ... I am ruined! For I am a man of unclean lips, and I live among a people of unclean lips, and my eyes have seen the King, the Lord Almighty" (Isaiah 6:3-5).

As we pursue worshiping in God's presence, our response to the revelation of His holiness and glory will be the same. The light of God's perfect holiness and the illumination that His presence brings reveals that we, like Isaiah, are utterly helpless, hopeless, and weak and share in the sinfulness of all of humanity. It is infinitely reassuring that God is still offering us what He did for Isaiah. In Isaiah's case, He sent seraphs flying down to gather a coal from His altar. "With it he touched my mouth, and said, 'See, this has touched your lips; your guilt is taken away and your sin atoned for'" (Isaiah 6:6-7). In our case, when we respond to the Lord's presence the way Isaiah did in contriteness and confession, God takes the blood of Jesus from His altar of sacrifice, the cross, and sprinkles it over us to purify us from our sins. For "If we confess our sins, he is faithful and just and will forgive us our sins and purify us from all unrighteousness" (1 John 1:9).

After he was purified from his sin, Isaiah tells us:

"Then I heard the Lord asking, "Whom should I send as a messenger to my people? Who will go for us?"

And I said, "Lord, I'll go! Send me."

And he said, "Yes, go . . ."

— Isaiah 6:8-9, NLT

Like He did for Isaiah, God offers us five things:
1. *An Invitation to experience Him in worship (Isaiah 6:1-2)*
2. *A Revelation of His holiness and glory (v. 3-4)*
3. *A Realization of our sinfulness (v. 5)*
4. *A Purification from our sin (v. 6-7)*
5. *A Commission to reach the world (v. 8)*

**The invitation to worship God is open to everyone.** The call to worship is universal. It is all around us. Creation itself beckons us to worship. Paul made the following statements concerning people who were about as far from living a life of worship as you can get, "For the truth about God is known to them instinctively. God has put this knowledge in their hearts. From the time the world was created, people have seen the earth and sky and all that God made. They can clearly see his invisible qualities—his eternal power and divine nature. So they have no excuse whatsoever for not knowing God. Yes, they knew God, but they wouldn't worship him as God or even give him thanks" (Romans 1:19-21, NLT).

Throughout the Bible, not only the invitation, but the mandate to worship God is clear, including the many verses telling us:

- Let everything that has breath praise the Lord (Psalms 150:6)
- Let all the angels worship him (Deuteronomy 32:43)
- The nations on every shore will worship him (Zephaniah 2:11)
- Worship the Lord in all his holy splendor (1 Chronicles 16:29)
- You must worship the Lord your God (Matthew 4:10)

**A revelation of God's holiness and glory comes to those who worship and seek him.** God will reveal His true self to those who worship Him in spirit and in truth. Like He did for

Moses, who said to God, "Show me Your glory," God will reveal Himself to us. When God's people were in a foreign land and had strayed from Him, Moses told them, "But if from there you seek the Lord your God, you will find him if you look for him with all your heart and with all your soul" (Deuteronomy 4:29). Wherever we are on our journey, whether near or far from the Lord, if we seek Him and worship Him, He will reveal Himself to us. When He does, we will see the perfection of His glory and holiness. This pure light exposes all that is within us and leads us to the next step.

**A Realization of our sinfulness.** We may be painfully aware of our utter sinfulness or we may think that we are a "pretty good" person. Regardless, we know that Jesus tells us that, "No one is good except God alone" (Luke 18:19). Paul reinforces this with, "There is no one righteous, not even one" (Romans 3:10). Once we accept that we are utterly hopeless in achieving right standing with God through our own goodness or efforts (self-righteousness), we can receive full forgiveness and access to intimacy with God through the righteousness of His Son. He was the one who tore the veil in two that separated us from intimacy with God. From there, we move to purification.

**Purification from our sins.** The passion and intimacy God wants us to have with Him can only exist in purity. God is pure and holy, and we need holiness beyond our own ability or righteousness in order to worship Him in spirit and in truth. The purity He provided for us through the cleansing blood of Jesus allows us to commune with God on the most intimate levels through prayer and worship. It allows us to freely and completely receive God's love and love Him in return. This defeats the enemy's plan to separate us from God. This is why Satan is so intent on leading us into impurity and defiling sins. This is why his battle plans are drawn around counterfeiting the best things God has to offer us: love, intimacy, worship, purity, relationship, and holiness.

Counterfeit experts know that the only way to recognize counterfeit currency is to thoroughly know the genuine. While we were in Nassau in the Bahamas recently, the street vendors had table after table of handbags for around $20 that sold for hundreds of dollars elsewhere. I sensed that some of them were "cheap" but basically had no clue. Trace, on the other hand, could tell right away when they weren't the real article. She had seen the real versions, she had picked them up in stores, and she had felt the quality and finish on the leather. She was much more prepared to recognize the counterfeit than I because she had spent time with the original.

Satan's counterfeits are easy to spot, if you know God's genuine articles. It's easy to be deceived by the world, the enemy and our flesh when we are not familiar with God, His Spirit, the mind of Christ, and His Word. Many people, even church folk, spend more time with the cheap counterfeits than with God's valuables. Like a drug dealer offering a quick high that will eventually bring you down, the enemy and the fallen world will constantly offer us lust instead of love, indiscriminate sex and pornography instead of intimacy, decadent music and arts instead of worship, selfishly using people instead of relationship, self-righteousness instead of God-righteousness, and pride and haughtiness instead of holiness.

David was a phenomenal worship leader who succumbed to inter-roof porn (watching Bathsheba on the rooftop), immorality (adultery) and even murder. In getting his life restored to God, along with confession of his sins, he declared, "I will set before my eyes no vile thing ... Men of perverse heart shall be far from me" (Psalm 101-3-4). He knew that to protect himself he would have to stop watching degrading, sensually enticing things and stop hanging around people who do. This is especially difficult for us creative artistic types who love movies, TV, other creative people, music, and surfing the net. Satan knows that and sets traps for us everywhere. So, in response we must hang out with people who encourage righteousness and purity as we fill our eyes, ears, and minds with "what is true and honorable and right [and] think about things that are pure and lovely and admirable. Think about things that are excellent and worthy of praise" (Philippians 4:8, NLT).

Even if we are engaged in worship with our spirit and soul, if we allow the carnal desires of our body to rule through sexual sin, then the enemy has prevented us from worshiping the Lord with all our heart, all our mind, all our soul and all our strength—our whole being—spirit, soul and body. (Mark 12:30)   But when faced with our own impurity we can respond like David did when his adultery with Bathsheba and murder of her husband were exposed:

> Have mercy on me, O God ... blot out the stain of my sins. Wash me clean from my guilt. Purify me from my sins. Create in me a clean heart, O God. Renew a right spirit within me. Do not banish me from your presence and don't take your Holy Spirit from me ... make me willing to obey you. Forgive me ... then I will joyfully sing of your forgiveness. Unseal my lips, O Lord, that I may praise you. Then I will teach your ways to sinners, and they will return to you.
>
> — Psalm 51, NLT

David is saying, "Touch my lips with Your purifying fire like you did for Isaiah, and then I will pursue You as he did." The rampant proliferation of sensuality and perversity in print, TV, movies, and the Internet has been used by the enemy to divert the passions God wants us to have in worship and in the context of God-honoring marriages.

The Message paints a powerful picture of either worshiping

with our bodies or wasting our bodies in immorality:

> Well, it may be true that the body is only a temporary thing, but that's no excuse for stuffing your body with food, or indulging it with sex. Since the Master honors you with a body, honor him with your body! God honored the Master's body by raising it from the grave. He'll treat yours with the same resurrection power. Until that time, remember that your bodies are created with the same dignity as the Master's body. You wouldn't take the Master's body off to a whorehouse, would you? I should hope not. There's more to sex than mere skin on skin. Sex is as much spiritual mystery as physical fact. As written in Scripture, "The two become one." Since we want to become spiritually one with the Master, we must not pursue the kind of sex that avoids commitment and intimacy, leaving us more lonely than ever—the kind of sex that can never "become one." There is a sense in which sexual sins are different from all others. In sexual sin we violate the sacredness of our own bodies, these bodies that were made for God-given and God-modeled love, for "becoming one" with another. Or didn't you realize that your body is a sacred place, the place of the Holy Spirit? Don't you see that you can't live however you please, squandering what God paid such a high price for? The physical part of you is not some piece of property belonging to the spiritual part of you. God owns the whole works. So let people see God in and through your body.
>
> – 1 Corinthians 6:13-21, The Message

I have seen numerous Christians, including worship leaders and team members, fall prey to the traps of immorality or substance abuse. It robs their spirits, souls, and bodies of life. We must learn to help exhort each other to purity and guard each other from impurity through genuine caring relationships of accountability. My fellow pastors and the men in my small group have agreed to ask each other the tough questions and promised to give each other honest answers. We have also agreed that if we fall even slightly that we will tell each other. The healthy fear of knowing that I'll have to tell my friends motivates me, but I know that the fear of rejection, judgment, or just plain embarrassment prevents many people from sharing their struggles or confessing their sins. I also know that some environments or relationships may not be safe, but in the context of a group of men or women coming together to share hearts and lives in accountability, I haven't seen anything but love, acceptance, and gracious understanding in response to people openly sharing their struggles.

When we maintain or restore our purity, we can have true intimacy with God. Like intimacy within marriage that brings about new life, intimacy with God does the same thing. In worship, we are impregnated with the heart, the love, and the compassion of God. As the image of Christ grows in us, we start to love what God loves and hate what God hates. This love for hurting, broken and lost people, along with the desire to destroy the works of the devil, causes us to reach out to bring new life to those around us and around the world. This creates new Worshipers who get captivated by the love of Christ and continue reproducing as well. From there, we move outwardly in our expression of our love to God.

**The Commission to reach the world. God intends to bless us so that we will be a blessing to others.** He says of Abraham, the founding father of our faith, "I will bless those who bless you ... and all peoples on earth will be blessed through you" (Genesis 12:2-4). Through worship, Isaiah experienced the life-changing manifest glory of God that led to his repentance and God's purifying touch. Added to his conviction and cleansing was his commissioning, God's call for Isaiah to reach those who weren't Worshipers yet.

God is commissioning us, like Isaiah, to take His word to the world until Christ returns and "all created beings in heaven and on earth—even those long ago dead and buried—will bow in worship before this Jesus Christ, and call out in praise that he is the Master of all, to the glorious honor of God the Father" (Philippians 2:10-11, The Message). At that point, missions will have completed its work. John Pipers states in Let the Nations Be Glad, "Missions exist because worship doesn't . . . When this age is over, and the countless millions of the redeemed fall on their faces before the throne of God, missions will be no more." Until then, worship can inspire us to make more Worshipers to fill the earth. If we cease to have spiritual children, we will cease to be a family in one generation. God wants us to be a part of His work to create spiritual babies who grow up and seek to have spiritual children of their own. The family of God is not a term we should take lightly. It is real and being a part of it is God's will for us.

We do this through worship and through living lives that reflect His love, acceptance, forgiveness, and redemption to those who are lost in a very spiritually dark and lonely world. Once we go through our Isaiah experience of invitation, revelation, realization, and purification, we are commissioned to help duplicate it in others. We are all called to spiritual reproduction, and God is very pointed in His question to us, "Who will go?" "Who will tell others about His intimate love and never-ending care?" Who will reassure the broken-hearted that God will never abandon them or leave them in their grief and sin?

## GO FOR IT

Many Christians have read these words and sensed God calling them into full-time ministry. Many more have read them and believed that the Lord was sending them to do His work right where they are—in their office, home, neighborhood and/or church. Wherever we sense a calling, God uses us when we avail ourselves to Him. But most of the time before this happens, He takes us on a journey of faith and preparation. It is a journey where we long to become more like Him and to spend our days living in the light of His glory.

God is preparing us as his bride for intimacy with His son to birth spiritual families that populate the earth. This is a restoration of His original intent. He created Adam and Eve for intimacy with Him and with each other. That relationship was breached with the veil of disobedience and sin. Through Jesus, God has lifted the veil and declared that intimacy has been restored so that His Son may now "kiss the bride." And in response, we offer ourselves fully to the one who has given His very life for us. As our whole being unites with Him through a life of worship, God blesses us and says, "Be fruitful and increase in number, fill the earth" (Genesis 1:28). And the whole earth is filled with His glory as we join with people of every tongue, every tribe and every nation to give praise to God with our entire spirit, soul and body in worship (Psalm 72:19; Revelation 5:9).

*Lord, I realize that I am on a journey that often follows along dangerous roadways where sorrow and difficulty cross, but you are my joy and my strength. (Nehemiah 8:10) I lift my eyes up to You and praise You because You are worthy of all my praise. Create in me a pure heart—one that can be used by You in your kingdom work on the earth so that others will come to know you as their Lord and Savior. Right now, I give my life to You as an offering as I commit to worshiping You all of my days with my whole spirit, soul and body. Amen*

## ABOUT THE AUTHOR

Joel Balin is senior pastor of CrossBridge Church in the metro Atlanta area. He has served as the Southeastern U.S. Vineyard worship overseer and was Worship and Arts Pastor at the Atlanta Vineyard for over a decade.

Joel has written for WORD Music and Inside Worship Magazine and served on the pastoral board of the group, Third Day. He has recorded, produced and performed with numerous CCM and worship artists along with companies and artists ranging from Michael Jackson to Sea World.

When not conducting worship conferences and seminars in the United States, Brazil, and Russia or mentoring worship leaders, Joel can be found at home in Georgia with his wife, Trace, and son, Robin, or visiting their daughter, Cecilia, in New York City.

## OTHER AMPELON TITLES

*God's Relentless Pursuit: Discovering His Heart for Humanity*
**by Phil Strout**
**retail price**: $14.95

Have you ever considered that instead of us chasing God, He is actually the One chasing us? In his book, author Phil Strout explores God's mission on earth and how His people join in His mission: to draw people into relationship with Him. Many common ideas and notions regarding our role in pursuing God are challenged as we discover the truth about what God is doing in and around us, both across the street and across the oceans.

Sample chapters and book are available for purchase at: www.ampelonpublishing.com

*Passionate Pursuit: Discovering the Heart of Christ*
**by Jason Chatraw**
**retail price**: $9.95

Do you want to experience a greater intimacy in the time you spend with God? If so, the devotional *Passionate Pursuit* helps set you on the right path. We must know that our relationship with God is a journey, not a quick trip. And being equipped for the journey will make it more fun and exciting.

Sample chapters and book are available for purchase at: www.ampelonpublishing.com

## OTHER AMPELON TITLES

*The Way In is the Way On: John Wimber's teachings and writings on life in Christ*
**by John Wimber**
**retail price**: $14.99

*The Way in is the Way* on is a compilation of the late John Wimber's teachings and writings on life in Christ. In classic Wimber style, he captures the heart of the reader by sharing practical applications from the Bible that result in life-changing experiences with God.

*Rediscovering the Power of Repentance and Forgiveness*
**by Dr. Leah Coulter**
**retail price**: $12.95

There is something deep within the heart of every man and woman that longs to see justice prevail. But what about when injustices are committed against us? How do we move forward? Can we really just forgive and forget?

Through a thorough examination of biblical teaching on forgiveness within the context of ancient Jewish culture, Dr. Leah Coulter dispels the notion that forgiveness is a one-way street. She explains the true depth of forgiveness and the freedom that results in a genuine heart of repentance. With personal stories and other examples, she gives readers a pathway to repentance and forgiveness, as well as showing them how to find healing and justice when they have been wronged by someone who has not repented.

Sample chapters and book are available for purchase at: www.ampelonpublishing.com

# NOTES

# NOTES

# NOTES

# NOTES

# NOTES

# NOTES

# NOTES

# NOTES